A Note From Rick Renner

I am on a personal quest to see a "revival of the Bible" so people can establish their lives on a firm foundation that will stand strong and endure the test when the end-time storm winds begin to intensify.

In order to experience a revival of the Bible in your personal life, it is important to take time each day to read, receive, and apply its truths to your life. James tells us that if we will continue in the perfect law of liberty — refusing to be forgetful hearers but determined to be doers — we will be blessed in our ways. As you watch or listen to the programs in this series and work through this corresponding study guide, I trust that you will search the Scriptures and allow the Holy Spirit to help you hear something new from God's Word that applies specifically to your life. I encourage you to be a doer of the Word that He reveals to you. Whatever the cost, I assure you — it will be worth it.

> Thy words were found, and I did eat them;
> and thy word was unto me the joy and rejoicing of mine heart:
> for I am called by thy name, O Lord God of hosts.
> — Jeremiah 15:16

Your brother and friend in Jesus Christ,

Rick Renner

Unless otherwise indicated, all scripture quotations are taken from the *King James Version* of the Bible.

Scripture quotations marked (*AMPC*) are taken from the *Amplified® Bible*. Copyright © 1954, 1958, 1962, 1964, 1965, 1987 by The Lockman Foundation. Used by permission. **www.Lockman.org**.

Scripture quotations marked (*NLT*) are taken from the Holy Bible, *New Living Translation*, copyright © 1996, 2004, 2015 by Tyndale House Foundation. Used by permission of Tyndale House Publishers, Inc., Carol Stream, Illinois 60188. All rights reserved.

A Life Ablaze

Copyright © 2020 by Rick Renner
8316 E. 73rd St.
Tulsa, Oklahoma 74133

Published by Rick Renner Ministries
www.renner.org

ISBN 13: 978-1-68031-618-6

eBook ISBN 13: 978-1-68031-656-8

How To Use This Study Guide

This ten-lesson study guide corresponds to *"A Life Ablaze: Ten Simple Keys To Living on Fire for God" With Rick Renner* (**Renner TV**). Each lesson in this study guide covers a topic that is addressed during the program series, with questions and references supplied to draw you deeper into your own private study of the Scriptures on this subject.

To derive the most benefit from this study guide, consider the following:

First, watch or listen to the program prior to working through the corresponding lesson in this guide. (Programs can also be viewed at **renner.org** by clicking on the Media/Archives links.)

Second, take the time to look up the scriptures included in each lesson. Prayerfully consider their application to your own life.

Third, use a journal or notebook to make note of your answers to each lesson's Study Questions and Practical Application challenges.

Fourth, invest specific time in prayer and in the Word of God to consult with the Holy Spirit. Write down the scriptures or insights He reveals to you about being filled with the Spirit and empowered by Him in your daily life.

Finally, take action! Whatever the Lord tells you to do according to His Word, do it.

For added insights on this subject, it is recommended that you obtain Rick Renner's book, *"A Life Ablaze: Ten Simple Keys To Living on Fire for God."* You may also select from Rick's other available resources by placing your order at **renner.org** or by calling 1-800-742-5593.

TOPIC

Stirring Up the Fire of God in Your Heart

SCRIPTURES

1. **2 Timothy 1:6** — Wherefore I put thee in remembrance that thou stir up the gift of God, which is in thee by the putting on of my hands.
2. **1 Thessalonians 5:19** — Quench not the Spirit.

GREEK WORDS

1. "stir up" — ἀναζωπυρέω (*anadzopureo*): to be enthusiastic, fervent, passionate, vigorous; to do something wholeheartedly or zealously; to rekindle or to stir back to life again
2. "quench" — σβέννυμι (*sbennumi*): to extinguish, smother, suppress, douse, put out, snuff out, or suppress; it most often means to extinguish a fire by dousing it with water; in some places, it means to evaporate or even to dry up

SYNOPSIS

God wants you to be a blazing inferno for Him for your entire life! You *can* stay spiritually on fire for Him in your heart. But it's up to you to stir up the fire of God inside you — and the way to do that is to *fuel the flame.*

If we don't fan the embers to maintain the flame of our spiritual life, eventually the fire in us will diminish. We must do something every day to feed our heart — to add the right fuel so that we can keep our hearts burning bright and hot for the things of God.

But even if your embers have gotten low, you can stir them up again until yours is *a life ablaze.*

The emphasis of this lesson:

We need to stir up the fire of God in us, but it is important that we use the right fuel to do that and to *stay* ablaze for Him. In these ten lessons,

Rick teaches on ten types of fuel necessary to stoke and sustain your spiritual fire — fuels you need to keep your passion for the Lord burning all your days on earth.

God wants us to be a flame of fire in the earth. But to do so, we must stay on fire as long as we live. Yet we can allow the disappointments of life, the busyness of work, wrong habits, and the distractions of success to divert our spiritual passion and reduce it to mere embers.

When the fire in your heart begins to wane, *you* must stir it up. This lesson will show you how!

In Second Timothy 1:6, Paul was speaking to Timothy, who was pastoring a church in Ephesus and going through a rough time. The church was under intense persecution by the Roman Empire, and Timothy saw that many people were defecting from their faith. Some leaders were leaving and others were embracing false doctrine, so Timothy was dealing with rejection and hurt — all of which affected him deeply, putting a damper on his spiritual fire.

Stir and *Repeat* — Fan the Flames and Then *Do It Again!*

Paul wrote to Timothy to encourage him, saying through the Holy Spirit, "Wherefore I put thee in remembrance that thou stir up the gift of God, which is in thee by the putting on of my hands" (2 Timothy 1:6). Paul was encouraging Timothy to *stir up* the gift.

The words "stir up" are from the Greek word *anadzopureo*. It's a compound of three words: *ana, zao,* and *pur.* The word *ana* means *to repeat an earlier action* — or *whatever you're doing, do it again.* The second word *zao* means *to be alive, lively, or thriving.* And the third word in this compound is *pur,* which is the word *fire.* You could translate the command to "stir up" as, "Repeat enthusiastically whatever you've done in the past to put life back into your spiritual fire. Be fervent, wholehearted, zealous, passionate, and vigorous about it."

In other words, stirring up the fire of God in your life is not something that just happens. You have to be *intentional* if you're going to successfully stir the embers and fan the flames of your spiritual life.

Timothy's fire was going out, probably because of all the issues he was dealing with. It was beginning to affect his spiritual passion. He felt like the flame in his heart was about to go out. That fire was burning low, and Paul said to him, "Timothy, it's time for you to quickly take action, and you're going to have to be intentional about it."

The word *ana* means, "What you did before, do it again." The word *zao* means, "Put life back into it." And *pur* refers to *the fire.* Paul was telling Timothy, "Do whatever you have to do to put the poker to the coals and to begin to stir them diligently. Whatever it takes, stir up the fire and the gift of God that's in you."

Well, if you want to have a big fire that burns brightly for a long time, you have to be faithful to continually put more fuel into the fire. If you don't pay attention to the fire, eventually it will go out. That's just the way that it works with fire.

An Early Lesson in Maintaining a Fire

In the program, Rick recounts an early lesson he and Denise learned about maintaining the fire necessary for living as they endured a bitter winter in the former Soviet Union. The following is an abridged account of their experience.

Before we moved to Moscow, we lived in Riga, Latvia, another region of the former USSR, and we found a very large apartment there to live in. It had 11 rooms, but it was located in a derelict building downtown. No one lived in the building except homeless people from the streets.

The first time I walked through that apartment, I noticed the crown molding, which was more than 100 years old, and several fireplaces, which were still so beautiful (there had been no central heat in that very old apartment).

But generally, the condition of the apartment was *hideou*s! There was graffiti written on the walls. The roof of the apartment building was caving in on one room. Not a single window had window panes; we had to replace them all. The floors were completely destroyed.

This apartment was so dilapidated that there was a hole next to the toilet that went all the way through the floor. Acid had formed a hole where men had missed the toilet over the years, and that substance had eaten through the floor, leaving a gaping hole through which we could see into the apartment below!

But I could see by faith what this place *could* look like, and because it was selling at the right price in its devastated condition, we purchased it and began putting it back into its original shape. When we were all done with the process, it was simply marvelous and in far better condition than it had ever been, even in its heyday. (And isn't that similar to what Jesus does with our lives after He has *purchased*, or *redeemed*, us? He seeks to restore what the devil stole from us.)

Part of the restoration process of this apartment was putting pipes in the walls so we would have heat in the winter. We were the only occupants in the whole building at that time and, of course, the first to install pipes suitable to conduct heat. This was just after the collapse of the Soviet Union, and the transitioning city officials had said, "If you'll put the pipes in by winter, we'll get heat to the building." Back in those days, no one had individual heating in his home. It was all centralized and came from the city. So we installed pipes as agreed, and radiators as well, and waited for heat. We did our part. But winter came, and the city did not do their part.

So Denise and I and Paul, Philip, and Joel were living in a fully restored apartment — in a completely derelict, dark, dingy building — with no heat! And although that apartment had *six* fireplaces, we didn't have fuel to place within them to produce any heat. And because of where we were located, getting fuel to where we were was nearly impossible.

Our family was at home in our apartment one winter day, wearing our heavy coats because there were only embers in the fireplace we'd lit in one fireplace (simply because we had run out of fuel). Suddenly Paul, Philip, and Joel rushed toward the front door, shouting, "We'll be back in a few minutes!"

Soon they returned, eagerly carrying into our apartment armloads of wood! I said, "Where did you get that!" They answered, "The apartment below us is in ruins, and like our floor when we moved in, the floor below cannot be fixed. So we decided to use that wood for our fireplace!"

They were right. The wood in the apartment below was warped or rotted and had come loose from the foundation so much that they as young children could pull the boards up with very little effort.

Denise and I watched in surprise as our boys began feeding 100-year-old wood into the door of that fireplace. And, *wow*, they really lit it on fire! Well, guess what? Fire began to burn once again in our home, and the fuel the boys retrieved from the apartment below provided heat for us that entire winter.

We were so thankful for the heat that fuel provided. But in order to maintain that fire and heat, we had to continually feed it fuel. If we didn't keep putting wood into the fireplace, eventually our fire would have gone out.

Similarly, if *you* are going to stay on fire for Jesus, you can't depend on the same fire you had years ago. If you don't do anything to the fire that was lit so brightly in your heart in the new birth, that fire you had for God in those early days will go out. In order for your fire to burn brightly for the Lord continually, for years and years to come, *you* are going to have to do something. You're going to have to keep adding the right kinds of fuel to your fire!

'Quench Not the Spirit' — Don't *Snuff Out* the Work of the Spirit in Your Life

You might say, "Tell me *exactly* what fuels I need to stay on fire so I can complete my spiritual race." That's what these lessons will cover. But first, read Paul's amazing words in First Thessalonians 5:19. He simply says, "Quench not the Spirit."

The very fact that Paul said, "Quench not the Spirit" means the Spirit can be quenched in your life. If you're not intentional concerning your spiritual walk, the fire of God in your heart can be quenched. Paul emphatically said by the Spirit of God, *"Don't do it!"*

The word "quench" is translated from a Greek word that means *to extinguish*. So this short verse could easily be translated, "Don't extinguish the

Spirit — don't smother, suppress, douse, or snuff out — the work of the Spirit in your life."

If you've ever sat around a campfire, you know that if you don't keep adding more fuel to that fire, the fire that burned so beautifully and brightly will continue to burn lower and lower until all that's left are a few logs and embers — charred remains of what once provided warmth, beauty, and even a means of cooking.

But the amazing thing is that even if all that's left to a once-raging fire are embers, if they're burning even a little, you can stir those embers and fuel them and restore the flames that burned so brightly.

What about your own life? If you feel your spiritual fire has begun to wane, there is great hope for you! You can stir the embers and add fuel to your flame. You simply have to be honest with yourself and not fall for the excuse many have used, saying, "Well, it's normal to be on fire earlier in your walk. But then as life goes on, that fire begins to die down."

But why would that line of reasoning be true? The Bible says God makes his ministers "a flaming fire" (*see* Psalm 104:4). It does *not* say, "They're flaming at first, but then they begin to wane"! No, a flaming fire is *a flaming fire!*

There is no doubt about it: God wants us to be a flame of fire — *a spiritual inferno* for Him — for the rest of our life! And what a way to meet Jesus one day — completely on fire for God! That's why we must identify our spiritual condition. We need to see if we simply need to maintain the fire that's burning in our life — and to perhaps turn up the heat and intensity of that fire — or if we need to stir the embers of a fire that has been diminished or that feels completely gone out.

It *is* possible to be *absolutely certain* that the flame of your heart keeps burning brightly as you continually stir up the gift of God inside you. That is going to be the exciting focus of this series!

STUDY QUESTIONS

Study to shew thyself approved unto God, a workman that needeth
not to be ashamed, rightly dividing the word of truth.
— 2 Timothy 2:15

1. What happened when you first gave your heart to Jesus? What did the Holy Spirit ignite in your heart (*see* Romans 5:5)? How did you cultivate that work of the Spirit and allow it to grow? Has that fervency abated? What does the Bible say about stirring up the gift of God?

2. Why was Paul exhorting Timothy in this manner at this particular time? Why was Timothy's flame of fire burning so low? In what ways does Timothy's plight apply to your own life?

PRACTICAL APPLICATION

> But be ye doers of the word, and not hearers only,
> deceiving your own selves.
> —James 1:22

1. When you first wake up each morning, begin fellowshipping with the Lord, praising Him and spending time in His Word if you're not already doing so. Keep a journal or notebook nearby to write what you learn or what the Lord impresses on your heart as you begin your day.

2. In what ways might a person quench the Spirit of God? Write down ways you can avoid that trap.

LESSON 2

TOPIC

Ablaze With God's Word

SCRIPTURES

1. **2 Timothy 1:6** — Wherefore I put thee in remembrance that thou stir up the gift of God, which is in thee by the putting on of my hands.

2. **Jeremiah 23:29** — Is not my word as a fire…?

3. **Jeremiah 20:9** — …His word was in mine heart as a burning fire shut up in my bones….

4. **Luke 24:15** — And it came to pass, that, while they communed together and reasoned, Jesus himself drew near, and went with them.

5. **Luke 24:27** — And beginning at Moses and all the prophets, he [Jesus] expounded unto them in all the scriptures the things concerning himself.

6. **Luke 24:31,32** — And their eyes were opened, and they knew him; and he vanished out of their sight. And they said one to another, Did not our heart burn within us, while he talked with us by the way, and while he opened to us the scriptures?

GREEK WORDS

1. "burn" — καίω (*kaio*): to ignite; to be set on fire; to burn; to be consumed with fire

SYNOPSIS

Do you want to be a blazing inferno for Jesus for the rest of your days on earth? Do you have regrets that it seems like you've lost the fire that you had earlier in life? *You can stir it up again!*

It's not enough just to begin a flame — you need to *sustain* it. In fact, if you feed that flame with the right fuels, that fire will be more than just sustained. It will grow stronger and stronger and brighter and brighter the longer you walk with God.

But what *are* the right kinds of fuel necessary to maintain this kind of strength and intensity for Jesus? In these lessons, we'll cover how you can stir up the gift of God in your life and *remain* ablaze with holy fervor by the power of these ten fuels:

1. The Word of God
2. Prayer
3. The Holy Spirit
4. Worship
5. Souls
6. Generosity
7. Holiness
8. Humility
9. Biblical Authority
10. The Fear of the Lord

In this lesson, we're going to look at the first and main fuel that will make all the difference in your spiritual life — the *Bible*, or *the Word of God*.

The emphasis of this lesson:

The Word of God is divine fire. And when you put the *Word* of God into your heart, you will burn with the *fire* of God, both now and for years to come.

In Second Timothy 1:6, Paul was writing to Timothy, whose flame was beginning to go out. His spiritual fire was being affected.

> **Wherefore I put thee in remembrance that thou stir up the gift of God, which is in thee by the putting on of my hands.**

The words "stir up" are from the Greek word *anadzopureo*. It's a compound of three words: The word *ana* means *to do something again*; the word *zao* means *to be lively*; and the word *pur* means *fire*. When you compound these three words, it means *to do what you used to do to bring life back to your fire*! The words "stir up" can be translated, "Be enthusiastic, fervent, passionate, vigorous," or, "Do something wholeheartedly or zealously."

Paul was talking to Timothy about putting his whole heart into fanning the flame of the gift of God inside him. First, this lets you know that if you're going to burn like a spiritual inferno, you're going to have to be very intentional about it. You can't just hope spiritual fire happens in your life. You have to be wholehearted and very zealous about putting spiritual fuel into your heart and stirring up, or rekindling and stirring back to life again, the flame that once burned brightly.

First Things *First*

The first fuel to add to your spiritual fire to build and maintain your fervor and intensity is the Word of God. If you want to be on fire for God, you have to be *ablaze* with His Word!

As we already saw, God's Word is fuel, but even more than fuel, it is *a divine fire*, absolutely infused with the presence of God Himself. And when you take the Word of God into your life regularly, it keeps your heart *ablaze*.

In Jeremiah 23:29, the prophet wrote, "Is not my word like as a fire…?" The Bible is not just a book that contains words — it is a book that holds the very presence, power, and the fire of God inside it.

The Bible itself is a fire. And when you take the Bible into your heart, it drives out darkness. It provides illumination. It brings warmth into the places of your life that have turned cold. It burns away dross. And it spreads its flames to others nearby. There's absolutely nothing to compare to the intense fire of the Word of God.

In Jeremiah 20:9, Jeremiah also wrote, "…His word was in mine heart as a burning fire shut up in my bones…." Once again, the prophet refers to God's Word as *fire.*

Have you ever taken God's Word into you and felt its fire doing its work? The Word of God will have a fiery effect inside your heart and upon your life if you give place to it and embrace it.

Luke 24 records the account of Jesus and the disciples walking on the road to Emmaus, where they didn't recognize the risen Savior, yet they were deeply affected by His presence and His words.

> **And it came to pass, that, while they communed together and reasoned, Jesus himself drew near, and went with them…. And beginning at Moses and all the prophets, he [Jesus] expounded unto them in all the scriptures the things concerning himself…. And their eyes were opened, and they knew him; and he vanished out of their sight. And they said one to another, Did not our heart burn within us, while he talked with us by the way, and while he opened to us the scriptures?**
>
> **Luke 24:15,27,31,32**

Their hearts *burned* when the Scriptures entered into them. The Scripture and spiritual fire are connected. And this word "burn" in verse 32 is the Greek word that means *to be ignited, to be set on fire,* or even *to be consumed with fire.* So you could actually translate the verse like this: "Did not our hearts feel ignited within us as He spoke about the Scriptures with us? Did not our hearts feel set on fire within us as He spoke God's Word to us? Didn't our hearts burn within us and feel consumed in a blaze of fire as He spoke?"

Jesus opened the Scriptures to these two disciples, and the result was their hearts were set *ablaze*. That's because the Bible is fuel, but even more than that, the Bible itself is divine fire. And when you take it into you, it ignites you and stirs you up.

Martin Luther said, "The Bible is alive. It speaks to me. It has feet. It runs after me. It has hands, it lays hold of me."

There truly is nothing like the Bible! It has a voice, and it speaks to you. It has feet, and it runs after you. It has hands, and it lays hold of you. When the Word of God is ingested into a believer, it releases its strength and convicting power. Its fiery power begins to transform that person from the inside out.

When you ingest the Bible, it literally unleashes the power of God and ignites a flame inside your heart. Just like when you put a match to kindling, when you put the Word of God in your heart, you will begin to burn with spiritual fire.

Seven Fiery Effects of God's Word on Your Life

The following are seven things the Bible will do in your heart that are a lot like the effects of fire.

Number one, as fire brings warmth, God's Word brings warmth and comfort in times of difficulty.

In difficult moments when you're wondering what you're supposed to do, opening your Bible, the Word of God with its divine fire, will bring such warmth into your life to comfort your heart and give you peace, strength, and hope.

Number two, as fire transforms an entire region where it is burning, God's Word transforms those who allow it to work inside them.

If a believer will allow the Word of God to enter his heart and allow the flames of God's Word to erupt inside him, his life will be transformed — *changed* — by the fiery power of God's Word. If that believer is willing to listen to the Scriptures expounded under the anointing of the Holy Spirit, his life will become conformed to the image of Christ and will never be the same again.

This is why the church you attend is so important. You need to be sitting under the teaching of the anointed Word. If a believer will take the Bible by faith into his heart, the supernatural power in that Word will be unleashed inside him. And when that power is unleashed inside him, it will transform him just like flames can transform any hill or countryside that is set on fire. Fire changes the landscape, and the fire of God's holy Word will change for the better the landscape of *your* life.

As you drill deep into the Bible, spiritual fire will be released deep within you. And when that happens, your heart, mind, will, emotions, and even your body, will be affected. From the inside out, your life can be transformed by the fiery effects of the Bible, God's fiery, glorious, eternal Word.

Number three, as fire has melting power, God's Word can melt any heart, even the stoniest, hardest hearts.

Maybe you have a heart that has become hardened in certain areas of your life. If you will expose those areas of your life to the fiery effect of God's Word, that Word will release its melting power into you. If you'll read the Bible and embrace it, taking it into your heart, it will begin to melt the stony places. If you've become cold, indifferent, or calloused, the fire of God's Word will melt those areas in your soul so that you once again will become soft and tender to the Holy Spirit and the things of God.

Number four, as fire burns garbage and debris, God's Word burns debris from our lives.

You have debris in your life — things you need to get rid of. You've tried to deal with it by yourself, yet it's still there. It keeps popping its head up over and over again.

But when you take the Bible into you, the Bible has the ability to burn away that unwanted debris. It really does burn up all the chaff that is left over in your soul from your former life. It burns up the chaff of sin and bad decisions. The Bible has the ability to burn that debris, or chaff, completely out of your life.

Number five, as fire is a purifier, God's Word will purify your soul and cleanse you.

Rick emphasized in the program that he is committed to reading his Bible as a part of his personal devotions to the Lord every day of his life. He reads it first thing every morning and refuses to eat food until he has ingested the Word, taking it into his heart and soul so that his life can be touched and changed by the fire of God.

When you take the Word of God inside you, it affects your mind. It renews your mind and purifies your thoughts. The Bible promises that its fire will do that work inside you, Psalm 119:9 says, "Wherewithal shall a young man [or anyone] cleanse his way? By taking heed thereto according to thy word."

In John 15:3, Jesus said, "Now ye are clean through the word which I have spoken unto you." And Second Corinthians 7:1 says, "Having therefore these promises, dearly beloved, let us cleanse ourselves from all filthiness of the flesh and spirit, perfecting holiness in the fear of God." We cleanse ourselves through the promises of God. Like fire, the Word cleanses our minds, including our memories.

Number six, as fire is a source of illumination, God's Word will illuminate your life and all your paths.

God's Word will be a light for you. It does what a lamp does in a dark room. When you "turn on" the Bible, suddenly you can see what you need to do. You can know how to make your decisions. That is why Psalm 119:105 says, "Thy word is a lamp unto my feet, and a light unto my path." And verse 130 says, "The entrance of thy words giveth light...."

The Scriptures are God's lamp. If you feel like you're sitting in a dark place and you don't know what to do, go to God's Word and receive it. Remember, the Bible itself is fire. And when the Scriptures come to you and enter into you, suddenly you have illumination. You can see what you previously could not see.

Number seven, as fire empowers mighty engines to operate, God's Word mightily empowers those who embrace it and believe it.

Mighty engines have to have energy — firepower — to operate. Similarly, when you take in the Word of God, which is fire, it releases divine energy and empowers you. God's Word can transform weaklings into giants!

Ecclesiastes 8:4 says, "Where the word of a king is, there is *power*...." When you embrace and act on the Word of God as His all-authoritative Word, He literally releases His power inside you. His Word divinely energizes you.

The psalmist said in Psalm 119:28, "…Strengthen thou me according unto thy word." According to this verse, when you ingest the Bible, it imparts power to you. It imparts to you energy and divine strength. There is nothing to compare to the Bible. If you feel like a weakling, take the fire of God's Word into you because it will transform you into a spiritual giant. If you feel that your fire is on a low burn, take the Scriptures into you, and they will release their fiery effect and cause you to come alive again with the fire of God.

The Bible has to be our primary, not our secondary, focus. It is the number-one, most important fuel of all fuels that you need to be continually adding to your spiritual fire.

The Bible is fuel, but the Bible tells us that it is fire itself. And when you take the Word of God into you, it releases all its fiery effects inside your heart. So if your spiritual fire is burning low, take the Bible into your heart. It will stir your "coals," it will stir up the gift in you, and you'll begin to burn brightly once again. And on a steady diet of God's Word, you will sustain your spiritual fire for years to come.

STUDY QUESTIONS

Study to shew thyself approved unto God, a workman that needeth not to be ashamed, rightly dividing the word of truth.
— 2 Timothy 2:15

1. How does the fire of the Scriptures strengthen you when you take it in? David knew that when he wrote in Psalm 119:28: "…Strengthen thou me according unto thy word." Recall a time when you had nothing else to lean on but the Word of God. Do you remember the scripture, or scriptures, you clung to? How did you apply the Word to help strengthen you to walk through that tough time?

2. Jeremiah the prophet wrote that God's Word was as a fire shut up in his bones. What did he mean by that statement? As fire in the natural burns garbage and other debris, how does the Word of God, when read, studied, and acted upon burn away things from our lives that need to be removed?

PRACTICAL APPLICATION

But be ye doers of the word, and not hearers only,
deceiving your own selves.
— James 1:22

1. What does it mean to you when you read the Bible and a word, phrase, or verse "jumps out at you"? You don't have Jesus to teach you Scripture firsthand, but He did bring you the Holy Spirit — a Helper, Advocate, Comforter, and Teacher. How do you inquire of the Lord concerning the study of His Word?

2. How has the Bible transformed you and your thinking so far? Can you write out or illustrate what He did with the fiery, melting power of the Word of God in your heart?

LESSON 3

TOPIC

Ablaze With Prayer

SCRIPTURES

1. **2 Timothy 1:6** — Wherefore I put thee in remembrance that thou stir up the gift of God, which is in thee by the putting on of my hands.

GREEK WORDS

1. "stir up" ἀναζωπυρέω (*anadzopureo*): to be enthusiastic, fervent, passionate, vigorous; to do something wholeheartedly or zealously; to rekindle or to stir back to life again

2. "continue" προσκαρτερέω (*proskartereo*): a compound of πρός (*pros*) and καρτερέω (*kartereo*); the word πρός (*pros*) means close, upfront, intimate contact with someone else; the word καρτερέω (*kartereo*) means to be strong, to be stout, to bear up, or to be steadfast; it pictures a strong, robust, "never-give-up" type of leaning toward an object

SYNOPSIS

Rick Renner is discussing how to make *and keep* your spiritual life ablaze for as long as you run your earthly race. Naturally speaking, you could build a fire that's like a raging inferno. But it is just a fact that a fire will go out unless more fuel is added to that fire. Your spiritual life is the same way.

Emphasis of this lesson:

If you want to keep burning for the Lord, you have to add fuel to your spiritual flame. And one of the fuels you need is *prayer*. When you really enter into prayer, it puts fuel on the spiritual flame in your life and it causes you to come ablaze with the power of God.

You might say, "Can I really be a spiritual inferno for Jesus?" Yes, you can. If you add the right fuels to your heart, you can build a fire that burns brightly, and you can sustain that fire so that it burns brighter and brighter the longer you walk with God.

The Bible says that God makes His ministers a flame of fire (*see* Psalm 104:4). If you're a child of God, that describes you. God wants you to be a flame of fire. That is the will of God for your life.

If you're not on fire for God, but you want to be, there's a way for you to do it. You just need to know how to reignite the flame that was kindled in your heart at the time you were born again — then keep that flame going for the rest of your life.

In a previous program, Rick talked about his family's apartment in their early days in the former USSR. They'd purchased an old apartment that had no heat for the first winter they were there. The apartment had fireplaces, but those fireplaces were empty. With no fuel in the fireplaces, they had no fire and no warmth.

That's a lot like believers who are "empty" and lacking in spiritual fire. They are going to have to add something to their heart to rekindle the fire of God that was placed there when they were born again. And just as the wood in a fireplace has to be stirred with a poker for the embers to be stoked and to stay ablaze, believers are going to have to keep themselves stirred up to fan the flame of spiritual fire placed in their heart by God.

Spiritual Fire Is Produced
by Applying Spiritual Fuel

Christians are a lot like a fireplace. They're the temple of the Holy Spirit, but if they're not adding any fuel to their life, they're not producing a lot of spiritual power.

Rick also discussed in a previous program that in order to reignite your spiritual flame and then maintain your fire for God, you have to be *intentional*. You have to look at your spiritual condition and evaluate it honestly. Then you have to open the door to your heart. If you find that your embers are on a low burn or your fire is about to go out, you're going to have to take action and begin adding the right fuel to your fire.

This kind of honest evaluation and intentionality is exactly what Paul exhorted Timothy to do in Second Timothy 1:6 when he told the younger minister, "I put thee in remembrance that thou stir up the gift of God, which is in thee by the putting on of my hands."

As seen in previous lessons, those words "stir up" is *anadzopureo*, a triple compound word in Greek. The word *ana* means *to repeat an action* or *to do something again*. The word *zao* is the word for *life* or *to be lively*. And the word *pur* is the Greek word for *fire*. But compounded, these three words form the single word *anadzopureo*, which in this context means *to do what you used to do to put life into your fire again*.

This means that if a lack of spiritual fire describes your situation, there is something you can do. You don't have to ask others to pray for you or to lay hands on you. You can do it yourself. You can add the fuel of prayer to your heart by yourself by simply taking the initiative and intentionally adding this fuel to the spiritual fire in your heart.

We've all had moments when our spiritual fire was at a low ebb, but we don't have to stay in that condition. We can change that by being intentional — by deliberately applying spiritual fuel to the embers in our heart and by fanning the flame.

Stir the Embers With the Fuel of Fervent Prayer

We've already seen that the first fuel to keep your life ablaze is the Word of God. The second fuel you need to remain spiritually on fire is *prayer*.

Prayer is an essential fuel to stir the coals of your heart. Leonard Ravenhill, the great prophetic voice said, "No man is greater than his prayer life...." That's already convicting, but it's really the truth. Ravenhill said, **"No man is greater than his prayer life. The pastor who is not praying is playing; the people who are not praying are straying. We have many organizers, but few agonizers; many players and payers, few pray-ers. Many singers, few clingers; lots of pastors, few wrestlers; many fears, few tears; much fashion, little passion; many interferers, few intercessors; many writers, but few fighters. Failing here, we fail everywhere."**

What an appropriate statement about prayer! Prayer is absolutely essential if we're going to remain an inferno for Jesus for the rest of our life.

Listen to these words in Jeremiah 33:3: "Call unto me, and I will answer thee, and shew thee great and mighty things, which thou knowest not." In this verse, we have God's promise that if we will call unto Him, He will answer us and He will demonstrate amazing, phenomenal power in our life.

When you look at the record in the book of Acts, you find that when the Early Church prayed, there was a torrential release of divine power. They called unto God, and God answered them and showed them great and mighty things.

Bible expositor A.C. Dixon said about prayer, **"When we depend upon organizations, we get what organizations can do. When we depend upon education, we get what education can do. When we depend upon man, we get what man can do. But when we depend upon prayer, we get what God can do."**

In today's world, we depend upon education, organization, machinery, etc. But we have largely failed when it comes to prayer; therefore, we don't see a lot of supernatural results. But the Early Church didn't have a lot of any of these things. But they had Jesus and Jeremiah 33:3! They believed that if they called on God, He would answer them and show them great and mighty things.

The great Wesleyan minister Samuel Chadwick said it like this: **"The one concern of the devil is to keep Christians from praying. He fears nothing from prayerless studies, prayerless work, and prayerless religion. He laughs at our toil, mocks at our wisdom, but he trembles when we pray."**

When you take prayer into your life, it literally stirs your embers and causes you to reignite your passion for Jesus.

The Book of Acts Isn't Just a History Book — It's a *Pattern* Book!

Many people view the book of Acts as a history book, and indeed it is. But it was not intended just to be a history book. The book of Acts is a *pattern* book. It shows us the pattern of how God worked then and how God wants to work in our life now and until the coming of Jesus. And when we come to that "pattern book," we find that the Early Church had a total dependency upon God. As a result, they experienced a torrential outpouring of God's power. They called unto God and God answered them and showed them great and mighty things. Their lives were literally *ablaze* because they called out to God in prayer.

Read, study, and consider closely the follow seven verses and passages from the pattern-book of Acts:

Acts 1:14

These all continued with one accord in prayer and supplication, with the women, and Mary the mother of Jesus, and with his brethren.

This verse is describing the 120 who had gathered in the Upper Room in Jerusalem waiting for the Day of Pentecost — and for ten days, they continued in prayer. They continued in supplication. In accordance with Jeremiah 33:3, they called out to God. God said through the prophet Jeremiah, "You call out to me, and I will answer you. I will show you great and mighty things beyond your comprehension." And they reaped the result in Acts chapter 2 when the Holy Spirit was poured out on the Day of Pentecost. God showed them great and mighty things!

Acts 3:1

Now Peter and John went up together into the temple at the hour of prayer, being the ninth hour.

Peter and John had gone to the temple to pray. And as they entered into the gate, there was a man lying there who had been sick since his birth (*see* v. 2). Peter and John began to call out to God in prayer, and just like Jeremiah 33:3 says, God answered them and showed them great and mighty things as this man, lame for all those years, suddenly jumped up and God's power was released (*see* vv. 7,8).

Acts 4:31

And when they had prayed, the place was shaken where they were assembled together; and they were all filled with the Holy Ghost, and they spake the word of God with boldness.

How would you like to be in a meeting where the very building you were in began to shake like a building in an earthquake because it was so invaded by the power of God? That's what happened in Acts 4:31. At that prayer meeting, they were praying in accordance with Jeremiah 33:3. They were calling out to God, and He answered them and showed them something amazing — the very building they were in was shaken by His power.

Acts 8:15,17

Who, when they were come down, prayed for them, that they might receive the Holy Ghost…. Then laid they their hands on them, and they received the Holy Ghost.

The Bible tells us that Philip had gone to Samaria and preached Christ, and people repented and there was great joy in that city (see vv. 5-12). Then Philip baptized them. Then the apostles came down from Jerusalem, *and when they prayed* for the people — calling out to God — those people who had been saved were then filled with the Holy Spirit. Gloriously, God showed them great and mighty things because they prayed!

Acts 9:10-18

And there was a certain disciple at Damascus, named Ananias; and to him said the Lord in a vision, Ananias. And he said, Behold, I am here, Lord.

And the Lord said unto him, Arise, and go into the street which is called Straight, and enquire in the house of Judas for one called Saul, of Tarsus: for, behold, he prayeth,

And hath seen in a vision a man named Ananias coming in, and putting his hand on him, that he might receive his sight.

Then Ananias answered, Lord, I have heard by many of this man, how much evil he hath done to thy saints at Jerusalem:

And here he hath authority from the chief priests to bind all that call on thy name.

But the Lord said unto him, Go thy way: for he is a chosen vessel unto me, to bear my name before the Gentiles, and kings, and the children of Israel:

For I will shew him how great things he must suffer for my name's sake.

And Ananias went his way, and entered into the house; and putting his hands on him said, Brother Saul, the Lord, even Jesus, that appeared unto thee in the way as thou camest, hath sent me, that thou mightest receive thy sight, and be filled with the Holy Ghost.

And immediately there fell from his eyes as it had been scales: and he received sight forthwith, and arose, and was baptized.

In this passage, we read that Ananias was praying. And as he was calling out to God, God spoke to him and said, "I want you to go to a street called Straight, to a house where there is a man by the name of Saul. Lay hands on him and pray for him, that he might be filled with the Holy Spirit and receive his sight." And the Bible tells us that in response to God's voice as he prayed, Ananias obeyed." He went to where Saul was, laid hands on the new convert, and you know the rest of the story; Saul later became the great apostle Paul.

Because Ananias prayed, he received direction from Heaven. He then obeyed and laid hands on a man who would become the legendary apostle Paul. God heard Ananais' praying and showed him, as well as the one he prayed for, great and mighty things!

Acts 10:1,2

There was a certain man in Caesarea called Cornelius, a centurion of the band called the Italian band,

A devout man, and one that feared God with all his house, which gave much alms to the people, and prayed to God alway.

This passage talks about a man by the name of Cornelius who feared God, along with the rest of his household, gave much alms to the people, and prayed to God always. Even though he was a pagan, he was seeking God, and Jeremiah 33:3 will work for anyone who prays. Cornelius was calling out to God, and God answered him. And God directed Peter to go to his house, and as a result of Cornelius' praying, the Gentiles experienced the first Pentecost. They were gloriously saved and filled with the Holy Spirit and spoke with other tongues. (*See* Acts 10:3-46.)

Acts 12:5

Peter therefore was kept in prison: but prayer was made without ceasing of the church unto God for him.

Peter had been locked up in prison, and a group of people were gathered in a house praying *fervently*, *robustly*, and *without ceas*ing for Peter's release. They were calling on God, and God answered. He sent an angel, and the angel set Peter free. Peter showed up at the house where people were praying for him, calling out to God. They were stunned because of the amazing thing that had been done in response to their prayers. But true to His Word, God showed them "great and might things" (*see* Jeremiah 33:3).

All over the book of Acts, from beginning to end, we find the Early Church praying and God responding to their prayers. As a result, we find a fervent Church *ablaze* as they were visited by the fire of God. God showed them great and mighty things, and that is God's promise to *anyone* who will add the fuel of prayer to his or her heart.

Prayer is simply powerful — so powerful that in Colossians 4:2, the apostle Paul said, "Continue in prayer...." That word "continue" is a compound of two Greek words: *pros*, meaning *to be up close, up front, or in intimate contact with*; and *kartereo*, meaning *to be strong and stout* or *to bear up and be steadfast*. When compounded, these two words form the new word *proskartereo*, which describes *someone that is strong and robust*, and it depicts *a "never-give-up" attitude*.

What Is the Object of Your Desire?

In other words, someone who is "continuing" has *a consistent, strong, never-relent-or-give-up type of attitude toward something*. That means that this phrase "continue in prayer" does *not* describe praying that's always done quickly. Rather, it pictures a believer (or a congregation of believers) who is tenaciously pressing into the things of the Spirit. That believer is leaning into it consistently, busily engaged in the activities that will bring the object of his desire to him.

This word "continue" pictures someone who is so determined that he consistently, vigorously presses toward the object of his desire. He is resolute and determined that he is not going to give up until he gets what he wants. This verse describes what our attitude should be in prayer. We have to press into it. We have to be determined and resolute.

This is why J. Oswald Sanders said, **"It is obvious that Paul did not regard prayer as supplemental, but as fundamental — not something to be added to his work but the very matrix out of which his work was born. He was a man of action because he was a man of prayer. It was probably his prayer even more than his preaching that produced the kind of leader we meet in Paul's letters."** Prayer was foundational to Paul's preaching, his epistles, and his entire ministry.

We have to understand that prayer is not just an add-on to life. It has to be a central fixture. R.A. Torrey said, **"We are too busy to pray, and so we're too busy to have power. We have a great deal of activity, but we accomplish little; many services, but few conversions; much machinery, but few results."**

We simply have to do what Jeremiah 33:3 says — call unto God, and call unto Him vigorously, robustly, and tenaciously, without giving up. And He will answer us and show us great and mighty things!

Oswald Chambers said, **"Unless in the first waking moment of the day you learn to fling the door wide back and let God in, you will work on a wrong level all day; but swing the door wide open and pray to your Father in secret, and every public thing will be stamped with the presence of God."**

Prayer releases the supernatural into our life. Prayer releases a torrential flood of God's power to us. Prayer releases all the answers we've been seeking!

Simply put, if we want to have God's mighty power — if we want to see mighty results — we have to do what Jeremiah 33:3 says: "Call unto me, and I will answer thee, and shew thee great and mighty things, which thou knowest not."

God really means that! It is a promise you can stand on!

STUDY QUESTIONS

Study to shew thyself approved unto God, a workman that needeth
not to be ashamed, rightly dividing the word of truth.
— 2 Timothy 2:15

1. The book of Acts records history — what else does it illustrate? What predominant theme was outlined for our benefit in the book of Acts? What happens when you have total dependency on God and on nothing else?

2. What happened when John and Peter went up to the temple to pray in the ninth hour? How did their timing and the outcome of their actions affect them as disciples and what they set out to do in prayer — as well as the lives of others? What happened when Ananias prayed as he was instructed to pay a visit to Saul? What was the far-reaching effect of that encounter?

PRACTICAL APPLICATION

But be ye doers of the word, and not hearers only,
deceiving your own selves.
— James 1:22

1. Think about how often Jesus went away to pray by Himself. Reflect on how your life is strengthened and illuminated through your own prayer life.

2. Remember that prayer is not simply an add-on to our daily to-do list. Consider ways that you are intentionally trying to grow in prayer. Do you belong to a prayer group? Do you set aside specific time to pray in the Spirit? If so, for how long? Do you pray the Word aloud? What does "pray without ceasing" mean to you?

TOPIC

Ablaze With the Holy Spirit

SCRIPTURES

1. **2 Timothy 1:6** — Wherefore I put thee in remembrance that thou stir up the gift of God, which is in thee by the putting on of my hands.

GREEK WORDS

1. "stir up" **ἀναζωπυρέω** (*anadzopureo*): to be enthusiastic, fervent, passionate, vigorous; to do something wholeheartedly or zealously; to rekindle or to stir back to life again

SYNOPSIS

The Scripture teaches us that when the Holy Spirit comes, He brings *spiritual fire*. In fact, the Bible says that when we're baptized in the Holy Spirit, we're baptized "with the Holy Ghost and with *fire*" (*see* Matthew 3:11; Luke 3:16). And if we're going to burn for God now *and keep burning for Him for years and years to come*, we need to experience the work of the Holy Spirit in our life continually. He adds the fuel we need to keep our life spiritually *ablaze*.

We've been looking at the fuels we must add to our heart if we want to stay on fire for God as we run our earthly race, and we've studied the fuel of *the Word of God* and the fuel of *prayer*. In this lesson, we're going to look at adding the fuel of *the Holy Spirit* to your spiritual flame.

The Holy Spirit doesn't just *bring* fire. The Scriptures teach us that the Holy Spirit *is* fire. The first time He shows up as the Holy Spirit in the book of Acts, He shows up with flames of fire. That's because the Holy Spirit is fire. And if you want to burn for God, you have to have the Holy Spirit actively working in this role in your life.

This lesson begins our study of the role of the Holy Spirit to bring spiritual fire to the life of the believer. We've seen that the words "stir up" in Second Timothy 1:6 — "...*stir up* the gift of God which is in thee..." — is a triple compound word in Greek. It is the word *anadzopureo*. The word *ana* means *to do something again*. The word *zao* describes *something that's alive or lively*. And the word *pur* is the word for *fire*. When you compound the three words, the new word means in this context, *"Do whatever you have to do to put life back into your fire again."*

These words in Second Timothy are intended for us to apply to our lives today. But the apostle Paul wrote them to Timothy by the inspiration of the Spirit because Timothy was going through a tough time, and his fire was beginning to burn low. He was dealing with serious problems that were distracting him from his calling. Paul said to Timothy, "Timothy, there is something you can do about this."

Notice Paul didn't ask someone to lay hands on Timothy or tell him to go for help. There's nothing wrong with that at times, but here Paul told Timothy there was something *Timothy* could do — and had to do — for himself. Timothy had to put the poker to the coals in his own heart. He could add the right fuels to his own flame to stir that fire back to life.

This is true for you today. *You* can bring life back to your spiritual fire if you'll intentionally keep the right fuels added and if you'll continually stir up the gift of God that's in you.

The emphasis of this lesson:

Believers are totally dependent upon the Holy Spirit in this life. *The Holy Spirit is fire.* He brought the fire of God to them, and He will be faithful to help God's people *keep* that holy fire burning brightly in their lives forever.

The Early Church understood this truth regarding their total dependency on the Holy Spirit and the fire He brought to them to do the work of the ministry and fulfill their calling and commission. Because they understood this so completely, they preached the saving Gospel to the ends of the known earth, cast out devils, healed the sick, raised the dead, and wrought miracles among the masses who needed a touch from God. Darkness was driven back, and the Church was ablaze because of the fire of the Holy Spirit in their midst!

Andrew Murray said, "**Men ought to seek with their whole hearts to be filled with Spirit of God. Without being filled with the Spirit, it is** utterly impossible that an individual Christian or a church can ever live or work as God desires."

Unfortunately, so much of the Church today operates without much supernatural activity of the Spirit at all. A. W. Tozer made the following statement along this line: **"If the Holy Spirit was withdrawn from the church today, 95 percent of what we do would go on and no one would know the difference. If the Holy Spirit had been withdrawn from the [early] New Testament church, 95 percent of what they did would stop, and everybody would know the difference."**

Some churches today believe in the supernatural activity of the Holy Spirit, but they don't see much of it in their church because they don't make room for it. Other churches believe the supernatural activity of the Holy Spirit ended with the age of the apostles. They believe in the work of the Holy Spirit to convict a sinner of sin and to bring that sinner to salvation. But after that, they don't really believe in the supernatural power of God or the gifts of the Spirit. They teach a lot of the Bible and are very sincere, but they don't understand the supernatural work of the Holy Spirit.

Donald Gee said, **"Doctrines about the Spirit are necessary and inevitable, but the all-important question is not what we mentally believe, but what we experientially enjoy."** It's important to know what we believe, but *we need to experience the power of God.*

D.L. Moody said, **"The fact is, we are leaky vessels, and we have to keep right under the fountain all the time to keep full of Christ, and so have fresh supply. I believe this is a mistake a great many of us are making; we are trying to do God's work with the grace God gave us ten years ago. We say, if it is necessary, we will go on with the same grace. Now, what we want is a fresh supply, a fresh anointing and fresh power, and if we seek it, and seek it with all of our hearts, we will obtain it."**

God wants to give you a fresh supply. You don't have to operate on a supply that you received a long time ago. Today if you'll seek with all your heart a fresh supply of the fire of the Spirit of God, He will make sure you have it.

With the Holy Spirit, There Is *Movement* and *Power*

In the last lesson, we saw that the book of Acts is a pattern book. But when you look at all the Bible, you'll see patterns, especially patterns about the way and the conditions in which the Holy Spirit moves.

In the beginning God created the heaven and the earth.

And the earth was without form, and void; and darkness was upon the face of the deep. And the Spirit of God moved upon the face of the deep.

Genesis 1:1,2

Because this is the first mention of the Holy Spirit in Scripture, it sets a precedent concerning a truth about the Holy Spirit that we need to know. In verse 2, we see the Holy Spirit is moving. And when you study the whole of Scripture, you find that when the Holy Spirit comes on the scene, He's always moving. And when He moves, something supernatural always happens!

From reading and studying the Bible, we can discern that the Holy Spirit is not silent or motionless. He moves. He speaks. He empowers. He moves upon people and circumstances, and they are changed.

We also see this in the life of Jesus — in fact, from Jesus' very conception. The Bible tells us the angel Gabriel appeared to Mary and said, "You're going to become pregnant supernaturally" (*see* Luke 1:31). Mary responded, "...How shall this be, seeing I know not a man?" (v. 34). The angel answered her, "...The Holy Ghost shall come upon thee, and the power of the Highest shall overshadow thee...." Gabriel said, in effect, "The Holy Spirit is going to move upon you, and power from on high will be released."

Of course, we know the angel was speaking of the virgin birth of Jesus the Son of God and Savior of the world into the earth. The angel finished, saying, "...That holy thing which shall be born of thee shall be called the Son of God" (v. 35).

The Holy Spirit is always in movement. He moved upon Mary, and she supernaturally conceived Jesus in her womb.

Years later when Jesus was baptized in the Jordan River, we see the Holy Spirit descending upon Jesus as a dove.

And Jesus, when he was baptized, went up straightway out of the water: and, lo, the heavens were opened unto him, and he saw the Spirit of God descending like a dove, and lighting upon him.

Matthew 3:16

The Holy Spirit *moved* on Jesus, and because He did, Jesus was empowered to begin three years of supernatural ministry leading up to His death and resurrection.

When the Holy Spirit moves, something always happens. Conversely, we find that if He's not moving somewhere, there is very little supernatural activity. The Holy Spirit is all about moving and acting!

Then in the book of Acts, we see the Holy Spirit in action (that's why it's called the book of *Acts*). His moving unleashed phenomenal amounts of power.

Let's look at it. Acts 1:8 where Jesus said to the disciples,

But ye shall receive power, after that the Holy Ghost is come upon you and ye shall be witnesses unto me both in Jerusalem, and in all Judaea, and in Samaria, and unto the uttermost part of the earth.

"...After that the Holy Ghost is come upon you and ye shall be witnesses unto me...."Jesus was prophesying a move of the Holy Spirit. Jesus said that when the Holy Ghost came upon them, they would be changed.

That word "power" is the Greek word *dunamis*, and it describes *explosive power*. It's the very word used to describe *the full might of an advancing army*, so Jesus was prophesying when the Spirit moves upon you, power is going to be released in you. The full force of God will march through you to advance upon the world. When the Spirit moves upon you...*wow!*

The power of the Holy Spirit isn't a quiet, reserved, motionless power. It is a real, explosive power.

We see the result of that was in Acts 2:4 on the Day of Pentecost.

And they were all filled with the Holy Ghost, and began to speak with other tongues, as the Spirit gave them utterance.

The Spirit moved into that Upper Room, and when the Spirit moved, something happened. Fire literally appeared in that place, and their hearts were set *ablaze*. They felt His presence and saw His fire. And they were empowered.

By the standards in most modern churches, we would say that what happened on the Day of Pentecost was pretty rowdy. Most people think the Holy Spirit is always silent and gentle. The Holy Spirit can be gentle, but when you study the book of Acts, you find that it was not always the case. Things got pretty shaken up when the Holy Spirit moved!

Acts 2:43 says that "many wonders and signs were done by the apostles." We saw several other references in the last lesson to "acts of the Holy Spirit" through the disciples.

Wherever the Holy Spirit is allowed to move, the supernatural acts take place. There is not an exception — from the beginning in Genesis and also in the book of Acts, and it's also true today. The Bible has set the precedent. When the Spirit moves, divine activity follows.

Hudson Taylor made this statement, **"Since the days of Pentecost, has the whole Church ever put aside every other work and waited upon Him for ten days, that the Spirit's power might be manifested? We give too much attention to method and machinery and resources, and too little to the source of power."** There's nothing wrong with methods. There's nothing wrong with machinery. There's nothing wrong with resources. We need all of it, but all of it is to no avail if we do not have the power and the fire of the Holy Spirit.

We have to be open to the moving of the Spirit. This is a fuel we must add to our spiritual fire. If there's no moving of the Spirit inside us, there's an element of divine fire that we will never know. So we need to open the door to our heart and make an honest assessment. We must ask, *Is there a move of the Spirit in my life?*

If you asked that question and the answer is no, you can make room for a move of the Holy Spirit in your life. You can add that fuel to your fire, because doing so will cause you to burn like an inferno for Jesus. When you add the fuel of the work of the Holy Spirit and allow Him to move, it will cause you to rage with spiritual power. That is what we see in the book of Acts — a pattern book to tell you what we should have in our life. It's undeniable — from beginning to end of the Bible, we find the movement of the Spirit of God. The Holy Spirit is not quiet and motionless. When He shows up, things take place.

We've already seen that you have to have the Word of God and prayer to keep your spiritual fire burning — to remain ablaze with passion for the things of God all your days on earth. In this lesson, we've seen that you also need the moving of the Holy Spirit in the fire of your heart in order to keep that fire burning brightly for the Lord. He's not theory, and He's not just doctrine. He wants you to experience Him in your life and to participate with the divine activity of Heaven through the power of the Holy Spirit.

STUDY QUESTIONS

Study to shew thyself approved unto God, a workman that needeth not to be ashamed, rightly dividing the word of truth.
— 2 Timothy 2:15

1. Look up the follow passages in Acts about the moving of the Holy Spirit. Write out the ones that mean the most to you personally. Acts 3:1-9; Acts 4:24-31; Acts 5:14-16; Acts 6:8; Acts 10:44,45; Acts 11:28-30; Acts 13:2; Acts 14:10; Acts 19:6; Acts 19:11,12

2. From your study of the scriptures from Acts listed in the first question, what are some of the conditions in which the Holy Spirit manifested Himself? What does it mean to wait upon the Lord?

PRACTICAL APPLICATION

But be ye doers of the word, and not hearers only, deceiving your own selves.
— James 1:22

1. What moving of the Holy Spirit have you experienced in life? Can you recall a time when there was no doubt that it was the Holy Spirit acting on your behalf to cause something or someone to change for the better?

2. Spend some time reading through John 14, 15, and 16 to see what these verses say about your relationship with the Holy Spirit.

TOPIC
Ablaze With Worship

SCRIPTURES

1. **2 Timothy 1:6** — Wherefore I put thee in remembrance that thou stir up the gift of God, which is in thee by the putting on of my hands.

GREEK WORDS

1. "stir up" — ἀναζωπυρέω (*anadzopureo*): to be enthusiastic, fervent, passionate, vigorous; to do something wholeheartedly or zealously; to rekindle or to stir back to life again

2. "worship" — προσκυνέω (*proskuneo*): pictures one who fell on the ground prostrate before a superior to worship or to collapse onto one's face or on one's knees in order to worship; worshipers who extended their arms toward a god in absolute love, affection, and devotion and even lovingly blew kisses toward that god; also, one who uses all available methods necessary to adore and worship a god

3. "temple" — ναός (*naos*): a temple or a highly decorated shrine; the image of vaulted ceilings, marble, granite, gold, silver, and highly decorated ornamentation; the most sacred, innermost part of a temple

4. "glory" — δόξα (*doxa*): pictures discernment, judgment, and splendor

SYNOPSIS

We all need to ask ourselves about the condition of our spiritual fire. Are we burning for God today like we used to burn? If not, we have to add fuels to the flame in our heart. We've already looked at the fuels of the Word of God, of prayer, and of the Holy Spirit. Another fuel we need in order to stay ablaze for Jesus for years to come is *worship*.

Emphasis of this lesson:

Worship is a spiritual fuel that every believer needs in his or life so he can be on fire — ablaze — for God for years and years to come. Worship is something you can do from your heart in your home, car, or *anywhere*,

because you are a walking sanctuary. And you need to join other believers in worship, where you as a congregation can experience a special manifestation of God's presence as He enters the atmosphere and begins to change everyone there.

The main text in these lessons is Second Timothy 1:6, which says, "Wherefore I put thee in remembrance that thou stir up the gift of God which is in thee by the putting on of my hands." Timothy was down. He was struggling, distracted by a lot of problems. And it was beginning to affect the fire of God in his heart. So when Paul wrote to him, Paul said, "Timothy, here's what you need to do. You need to stir up the fire of God, the gift of God, that is in you."

In previous lessons, we saw in detail the definition of "stir up." These words also mean to be enthusiastic, fervent, vigorous, or passionate — to do something wholeheartedly or zealously. We know from this definition that to cause your spiritual fire to burn brighter or to rekindle that fire again, you have to be very intentional. You have to assess the condition of your fire and identify the fuels you need to add to keep your fire burning brightly.

In this lesson, we're talking about worship. When a person worships, it opens a channel through which the presence of God enters his or her atmosphere. In a church, when real, bona fide worship occurs, it forms a conduit through which the presence of God enters the atmosphere. And when that presence of God comes, everything can be changed. Mindsets can be shifted. And it is amazing how God can convict a person about the way he's thinking or living during a time of worship. Revelation can be unlocked during a time of worship. Deliverance and healing can come. Rick stated in the program that the concept for almost every book he has written has come to him during times of worship. He said it's like God suddenly opened the spirit realm and downloaded the information into him.

There's nothing that can compare to what takes place during a time of worship when the presence of God literally charges the atmosphere. That presence is so powerful that it can change everyone in the place. *Things change when God's presence permeates the scene!*

Worship leader and author Matt Redman said about worship, "So often when my worship has dried up, it's because I haven't been fueling the fire. I haven't set aside any time to soak myself under the showers of God's revelation. Often, time is the key factor. But if we can find space to soak ourselves in God's Word, His presence, His creation and spend time with other believers, then we'll find that the revelation floods back into our lives; and our hearts will respond with a blaze of worship once more."

A. W. Tozer said, "I can safely say, on the authority of all that is revealed in the Word of God, that any man or woman on this earth who is bored and turned off by worship is not ready for heaven." That's because Heaven is going to be filled with *worship*!

Theologian Karl Barth said about worship: "Worship is the most momentous, the most urgent, the most glorious action that can take place in human life." That's because it gets us ready for what's to come.

There's a whole realm of God that is only revealed to us during worship.

What Is New Testament Worship?

Many ask the question, "What exactly *is* worship?" That's a very important question, and to answer it, it is wise to study what worship is *not*. In the program, Rick related the following story, in effect, to illustrate what worship *isn't*.

> In the very heart of Moscow, right near the Kremlin, is a very famous theater called the Bolshoi Theater. Some of the greatest opera, music, and ballet in the world is performed on the stage of the Bolshoi Theater.
>
> What takes place on that stage is amazing. That stage is a stage of human achievement. People scream with applause. Others are dumbfounded at the amazing talent they witness. But as wonderful as all that is in terms of human achievement, it does not provide a channel or conduit through which the presence of God can enter in. The Bolshoi Theater is about talent and achievement.
>
> Even in the Church, good music and good choreography do not produce worship. Music can come from the fingers. It can come from the soul. It can be excellent (and in the Church, it *should* be excellent because we're the people of God; we should provide

the best). But in itself, talent and achievement do not constitute worship.

In our own church, we have people playing on our platform who have also performed in the Bolshoi Theater. We have some of the very best singers and musicians, and they rehearse to give their very best because it is for the Lord. But just playing from your fingers and from your soul does not necessarily mean you're worshiping God. Real worship is not about human achievement or human talent. Real worship occurs when you worship *from the heart.*

When real worship occurs, it forms a channel or a conduit through which God Himself enters into a congregation with His presence. Or He can enter the atmosphere of the worshiper himself. Worship is supernatural. When God's presence comes, things happen.

So what does the word "worship" mean in the New Testament? It was translated from the Greek word *proskuneo,* and it describes *one who fell prostrate on his face before a superior in order to worship.* It also means *to collapse onto one's face or on one's knees in order to worship.*

Remember, one definition of "worship" from the Greek is *to lovingly blow kisses toward the object of one's worship* and *to use all available methods to adore and worship.* Worshipers who extend their arms upward — and even lovingly "blow kisses" — to God in absolute love, affection, and devotion are using all resources available to them to worship and adore Him.

So when you're worshiping God — and one of those definitions is *to blow kisses* — you are experiencing a very intimate moment in which you're focusing solely upon God, not on human talent. Human talent might help you get into that place of intimacy in your worship of God. But worship is not about human achievement — it is about creating an atmosphere in which God can inhabit and move.

We are the temple of the Holy Spirit (*see* 1 Corinthians 6:19), which means you don't even have to go to a church building for this to take place. It can happen right where you are. Of course, there's a special anointing that happens when you're joined corporately with other believers, but you can worship the Lord privately as well.

What? know ye not that your body is the temple of the Holy Spirit?

1 Corinthians 6:19

That word "temple" is the Greek word *naos,* which describes *a temple or a highly decorated shrine.* It portrays the image of vaulted ceilings, marble, granite, gold, silver, and highly decorated ornamentation. It also describes *the most sacred, innermost part of a temple.*

Remember that Paul was writing to people who had been pagans. And in the pagan world there were temples everywhere. If you were visiting Rome, Athens, or Ephesus, and so on during that time, you would see magnificent temples. Entering the innermost courts of a shrine, you would have seen marvelous, precious stones and ornamentations of gold and silver, as well as luxurious fabrics. The interiors of these temples were fabulous to behold.

You Are God's Glorious Sanctuary!

Paul deliberately used the word *naos* to communicate his Spirit-inspired message. There were many temples in Corinth. When Paul used this word, he knew it would conjure a certain image in the minds of his readers. The apostle was saying to them, "If your eyes could be opened and you could see your spiritual interior, you would find that God has constructed something magnificent within you. In the new birth, your spirit was re-created, and your interior is now highly ornamented with the gifts of the spirit and the fruit of the spirit and other precious, godly things placed there by Him."

In fact, what God did in us was so magnificent that the Holy Spirit said, "I want to live inside that person." The Holy Spirit is inside you. If you could see what is in you, it would give such a boost to your self-image. *You are the temple of the Holy Spirit!*

At the moment of your new birth, you became a walking sanctuary. Ravi Zacharias said it like this: "The Christian does not go to the temple to worship. The Christian takes the temple with him or her. Jesus lifts us beyond the building and pays the human body the highest compliment by making it His dwelling place, the place where He meets with us."

This means as temples of the Holy Spirit, we are the sanctuary of God — which further means we can worship anywhere we are — in our homes, cars, at church, on the street, etc.

You are the sanctuary of God Himself!

God Responds to True Worship

But who are we worshiping? We're worshiping God! Worship is not about us or our talents and skills, but about *Him.* Talent may help us enter His manifest presence, but worshiping in God's presence is about Him and His goodness, His holiness, and His magnificence.

Worship occurs when we reach a point of abandonment and surrender — when we're totally focused on God. And when we do this according to the usage of the Greek word *proskuneo,* translated as "worship," we are intimately "blowing kisses" to God. We are drawing near to Him in adoration, adulation, and complete submission, awe, and abandonment. And in that moment, our worship becomes a conduit or a channel through which God enters our atmosphere or surroundings, filling it with His life-changing presence.

How does God respond to this kind of worship? The answer is in Psalm 22:3, which says, "…Thou art holy, O thou that inhabitest the praises of Israel." That word "inhabitest" or "inhabits" is a Hebrew word that means *to sit enthroned.* It pictures God sitting or resting on top of a person or congregation that is taken in the worship of Him.

When we abandon ourselves from our hearts in focused concentration on Him, it's as if God says, "I want to be a part of that." And His presence comes and *inhabits* or *sits in the midst of* the true worship of Him. His presence hovers over a person or congregation that is in true worship of the Almighty.

In this program, Rick shared the following memory of God's manifested presence in Kathryn Kuhlman meetings he attended as a young person.

> Kathryn Kuhlman's meetings were amazing. Kathryn Kuhlman understood worship and that when worship was taking place, the presence of God came. In fact, Kathryn Kuhlman never entered an auditorium or stood on a stage until people had first been worshiping.

I can remember sitting in those meetings, and the crowds were caught up in rapturous worship, totally caught up in the presence of God. And before Kathryn Kuhlman was ever on the stage, you could already feel the power of God moving upon the auditorium. She simply stepped into an environment where God was already working. The presence of God was hovering on top of those auditoriums of people. The Spirit of God was already moving because when you worship, God hovers. He sits enthroned on top of worshiping people.

God's Manifested Glory in Worship

There's something else that's very important about the worship of God. His glory comes when He is worshiped. The Old Testament describe this in depth. It describes the glory as something that is "heavy" or weighty. The book of Second Chronicles tells us when the priests entered the temple, they couldn't even stand because of the glory cloud (*see* 2 Chronicles 5:14). In other words, the manifested glory of God was so weighty that they literally collapsed underneath it.

In the New Testament, the word "glory" is translated from the Greek word *doxa*, which describes *discernment, judgment,* or *splendor.* It is the splendorous presence of God that is hovering above a person or congregation that makes room for the glory of God and the mind of God. And the Holy Spirit, who is in the midst of that glory, begins to discern every single need present.

Even in the midst of a large congregation, in the glory, the Holy Spirit begins judging or discerning the needs in each individual's life. In that environment, the Spirit of God begins to meet every person according to his need. If a person needs conviction of sin, in the glory, that person is convicted. If someone needs healing or deliverance, in the presence of that glory, the Spirit of God begins to move, and the person can receive his need met for healing or deliverance. If someone needs wisdom or revelation, it's amazing how a person's mind can be opened and he can see what he was never able to see before! That's because the person is in God's environment of light.

All of this and more can take place in an environment where God has come to manifest His glory and presence!

C. S. Lewis said, "In the process of being worshiped, God communicates his presence to men." When we worship and the glory of God comes, it is "heavy" with everything good, including all of God's goodness. That presence is filled with miracles. It's filled with deliverance. It's filled with gifts of the Holy Spirit. And the Holy Spirit begins discerning what is needed by every person present. And He thusly begins distributing according to the need. The atmosphere of worship is a miraculous, supernatural environment where God's presence and glory are manifested and people's lives are *changed*.

Worship is a spiritual fuel that every believer needs in his or life so he can be on fire — ablaze — for God for years and years to come. Worship is something you can do from your heart in your home, car, or *anywhere*, because you are a walking sanctuary. And you need to join other believers in worship, where you as a congregation experience a special presence of God, and He literally enters the atmosphere with His presence and begins to change everyone there.

If you feel that your fire is burning low, throw another log on the fire or stir up those dwindling embers and begin to worship God right now. His presence will come and ignite a new flame in your heart so that you can continue to burn brightly for Him as you run your spiritual race on earth.

STUDY QUESTIONS

**Study to shew thyself approved unto God, a workman that needeth
not to be ashamed, rightly dividing the word of truth.
— 2 Timothy 2:15**

1. You may have had an idea of what worship is, but what did you learn in this lesson that worship is *not*?
2. What does it mean that "God inhabits the praises of His people"?
3. The New Testament Greek word for "glory" is *doxa*. Explain what that means, as well as its practical application when a person or a congregation worships God.

PRACTICAL APPLICATION

**But be ye doers of the word, and not hearers only,
deceiving your own selves.
— James 1:22**

1. Have you engaged in the corporate worship of God in your church? Do you make sure you're at church on time so that you can enter into worship as soon as the service starts?

2. Worship is more than singing beautiful songs. It is even more than instruments and music. What are your observations of true worship versus just talent as a singer or musician?

3. Practice reading the Psalms out loud to yourself. Learn to express your own heart toward Him in dependency and trust. Write down what you learn or experience from Him during those times.

TOPIC

Ablaze With Generosity

SCRIPTURES

1. **2 Timothy 1:6** — Wherefore I put thee in remembrance that thou stir up the gift of God, which is in thee by the putting on of my hands.

2. **Matthew 6:21** — For where your treasure is, there will your heart be also.

3. **Acts 10:38** — How God anointed Jesus of Nazareth with the Holy Ghost and with power: who went about doing good, and healing all that were oppressed of the devil; for God was with him.

4. **John 12:5** — Why was not this ointment sold for three hundred pence, and given to the poor?

5. **Acts 2:42,43** — ...They continued steadfastly in the apostle's doctrine and fellowship, and in breaking of bread, and in prayers. And fear came upon every soul: and many wonders and signs were done by the apostles.

6. **Acts 2:44,45** — And all that believed were together, and had all things common; and sold their possessions and goods, and parted them to all men, as every man had need.

7. **Acts 4:3** — And when they had prayed, the place was shaken where they were assembled together; and they were all filled with the Holy Ghost, and they spake the word of God with boldness.

8. **Acts 4:32** — And the multitude of them that believed were of one heart and of one soul: neither said any of them that aught of the things which he possessed was his own; but they had all things common.

9. **Acts 4:33-35** — And with great power gave the apostles witness of the resurrection of the Lord Jesus: and great grace was upon them all. Neither was there any among them that lacked: for as many as were possessors of lands or houses sold them, and brought the prices of the things that were sold, and laid them down at the apostles' feet: and distribution was made unto every man according as he had need.

10. **Luke 6:38 (*NLT*)** — …Your gift will return to you in full — pressed down, shaken together to make room for more, running over, and poured into your lap. The amount you give will determine the amount you get back.
    2 Corinthians 9:6 — He which soweth sparingly shall reap also sparingly; and he which soweth bountifully shall reap also bountifully.

11. **Philippians 4:19** — But my God shall supply all your need according to his riches in glory by Christ Jesus.

12. **Philippians 4:19 (*RIV*)** — But my God will supply your needs so completely that He will eliminate all your deficiencies. He will meet all your physical and tangible needs until you are so full that you have no more capacity to hold anything else. He will supply all your needs until you are totally filled, packed full and overflowing to the point of bursting at the seams and spilling over.

GREEK WORDS

1. "stir up" — ἀναζωπυρέω (*anadzopureo*): to be *enthusiastic, fervent, passionate, vigorous*; to do something wholeheartedly or *zealously*; to rekindle or to stir back to life again

2. "doing good" — εὐεργετέω (*euergeteo*): pictures a benefactor, a philanthropist, one who financially supports charitable works; one who uses his financial resources to meet needs of disadvantaged people; used in connection with the provision of food, clothes, or some other commodity associated with physical or material needs

SYNOPSIS

The fuels covered in this series are as follows:

- **The Word**
- **Prayer**
- **The Holy Spirit**
- **Worship**
- **Generosity**
- **Holiness**
- **Humility**
- **Fear of the Lord**
- **Souls**

In this series so far, we've looked at the Word of God, prayer, the Holy Spirit, and worship as "passions" that a believer must add consistently to his spiritual fire if he is to remain fervent and devoted concerning the things of God.

In this lesson, we're studying *generosity* as one of the fuels you need to stay on fire for God as you run your earthly race on the earth. In this segment, you will see that the Early Church was generous toward God, and as a result, He was generous toward them — in finances, in protection, in a generous supply of His Spirit, and in every way imaginable.

Emphasis of this lesson:

It is just a fact that when you give from your heart, your life is set *ablaze*. A generous spirit literally fuels the spiritual flame in your heart.

This lesson is not "just another message on giving." It is a message of fueling the spiritual flame that was brightly lit in your heart at the time of your new birth. The apostle Paul wrote by the inspiration of the Spirit, "Wherefore I put thee in remembrance that thou *stir up* the gift of God, which is in thee by the putting on of my hands" (2 Timothy 1:6). To fan the flame of your spiritual life is something *you* have to do. But Jesus set the example and has made every provision for you to follow in His steps. Today He stands ready to help you stir the embers, fan the flame, and live *impassioned* and *ablaze* with His glory in your spiritual walk.

Money Is a Revealer of the Heart

A heart on fire is a generous heart. Songwriter Amy Carmichael said, **"You can give without loving, but you cannot love without giving."** When we love someone, we naturally want to give to them.

Giving is an issue of the heart. Jesus said, "For where your treasure is, there will your heart be also" (Matthew 6:21). Based on this verse, it's not difficult to determine what a person really loves. According to Jesus, if you follow a person's money, that is where his heart is.

When you love the Lord, you give to the Lord. When you love your spouse, you give to your spouse. Where your heart is, that is where you put your resources of money, time, and attention. It's where you place your passion.

Theologian Stephen Olford wrote: **"I am convinced that the devil has caused the subject of giving to stir up resistance and resentment among God's people because he knows there are few ways of spiritual enrichment like the exercise of faithful stewardship."**

It takes money to operate in this life. For example, if you go to the theater, before they will issue you a ticket, they ask for *money*. When you go a restaurant, after you enjoy your meal, the end of that experience is your bill! Everywhere you go, people are, in effect, asking for *money, money, money*!

So why does it surprise so many people that God would address this issue of money? Money is very important. As we saw, *money is a revealer of the heart*. Where your treasure is, that is exactly where your heart is. In fact, the subject of money is so important that Jesus spoke about money more than any other single topic He ever addressed during His ministry.

Jesus the Great Philanthropist

D. L. Moody said, **"When God gave Christ to this world, He gave the best He had, and He wants us to do the same."** God is a very generous God, and He is generous with those who are generous. It makes sense that Jesus would have displayed generosity in His earthly ministry, because He was the image of the Father (*see* John 14:9).

Acts 10:38, a very familiar verse to most, further proves this point of Christ's generosity.

> **How God anointed Jesus of Nazareth with the Holy Ghost and with power: who went about doing good, and healing all that were oppressed of the devil; for God was with him.**

Of course this verse describes the healing and delivering ministry of Jesus. But this phrase "doing good" emphasizes Jesus' generosity in the area of giving and, in particular, giving physical resources to meet real physical needs.

Many think the words "doing good" are a clarification of Christ's anointing to heal the sick, raise the dead, and deliver those who were oppressed and possessed by demons. But these words in the Greek exactly describe *a philanthropist* or *a benefactor.* They depict *one who financially supports charitable works* or *one who uses his financial resources to meet the needs of disadvantaged people.* It is used in connection with *the provision of food, clothes, or some other commodity associated with physical or material needs.*

The same verse that discusses Jesus' healing, and delivering ministry also discusses Jesus' ministry to meet the needs of people who were disadvantaged in some way. In other words, there was one part of Jesus ministry that was philanthropic. *Jesus was a giver.*

We know Jesus had a lot of money available in His ministry — so much that He had a treasurer. In John 12, we read the account of Mary coming to Jesus and pouring spikenard on His feet, which was very costly and valuable. Judas, who was Jesus' treasurer, said, "Why was not this ointment sold for three hundred pence and give to the poor?" (v. 5).

Once can infer from this verse that Jesus had a ministry to the poor. And now we know from Acts 10:38 that, in addition to supernaturally healing people's bodies, Jesus met the physical, tangible needs of people through a philanthropic part of His ministry, which means Jesus was generous. He used His funds to meet the needs of other people. Jesus was the image of the Father. The Father is generous, so of course Jesus was going to be generous in His earthly ministry because He demonstrated the Father to us (*see* John 5:19).

You Can't *Out-Give* God!

Then when you come to the early New Testament Church after Christ's resurrection, you find that generosity also flowed in the Church. God is generous, and when God is working among people, they become generous too. Their hearts open to Him, and when their hearts open, they open their resources, and they begin to give like Him and in response to Him.

You begin to give when the fire of God is working in your heart, because that fire inspires you to act like He acts. In fact, it is amazing how responding to Him in generosity triggers a cycle between giving and demonstrations of the fire and glory of God.

Acts 2:42-45

And they continued steadfastly in the apostles' doctrine and fellowship, and in breaking of bread, and in prayers.

And fear came upon every soul: and many wonders and signs were done by the apostles.

And all that believed were together, and had all things common;

And sold their possessions and goods, and parted them to all men, as every man had need.

When God's power erupted among the people and set them on fire, they began to open their wallets because they were totally sold out to Jesus. It was as if they said, "Lord, everything we have is Yours. We are not holding back, hanging on to what we have. Whatever we have, if You need it, Lord, it's Yours." This kind of surrender is evidence of hearts on fire.

Acts 4:31,32

And when they had prayed, the place was shaken where they were assembled together; and they were all filled with the Holy Ghost, and they spake the word of God with boldness.

And the multitude of them that believed were of one heart and of one soul: neither said any of them that ought of the things, which he possessed, was his own; but they had all things common.

When the Holy Spirit moved among them, instead of their being stingy and hoarding their possessions, they surrendered themselves completely to the Lord.

We see a pattern in the pattern-book of Acts that the fire of God inspired generosity and giving, which ignited supernatural power and demonstrations.

Acts 4:33-35

And with great power gave the apostles witness of the resurrection of the Lord Jesus: and great grace was upon them all.

Neither was there any among them that lacked: for as many as were possessors of lands or houses sold them, and brought the prices of the things that were sold,

And laid them down at the apostles' feet: and distribution was made unto every man according as he had need.

When the fire of God was moving among them, their hearts began to open. They were so on fire with the power of God that when their hearts opened, their resources opened to Him, and they said, in effect, "Lord, whatever we have is Yours with nothing held in reserve."

In this program, Rick shared the testimony of an old denomination church that he and Denise were a part of. The church was more than 100 years old, and God had moved mightily in that church in its early history. But over the years, the tone had become very rigid and stale. Then the pastor began preaching on giving. At first, the people were not very receptive, but he kept teaching the Word, especially the scriptural principle that money shows the motive of the heart (*see* Matthew 6:21). Your treasure really does demonstrate where your heart is.

Finally, that congregation really began to "hear" the pastor's message. And they began to have a giving campaign in their church. The growing offerings were evidence that the fire of God was really catching in that church. They had opened their hearts and had begun giving into the work of God, demonstrating their love for Jesus. And it triggered the fire of God and a move of the Spirit. Suddenly, the joy of the Lord filled that church, miracles filled that church, and the altars were packed with people getting saved. This was a direct result of a stingy church becoming generous. When that church became generous with God, God became very generous with that church. He poured His Spirit out upon that congregation. They reaped what they sowed before their very eyes.

When *you* are generous with God, God will be generous with you. This is what the Scripture teaches.

> **Give, and you will receive. Your gift will return to you in full — pressed down, shaken together to make room for more, running over, and poured into your lap. The amount you give will determine the amount you get back.**
> **Luke 6:38 (*NLT*)**

> **He, which soweth sparingly, shall reap also sparingly; and he, which soweth bountifully, shall reap also bountifully.**
> **2 Corinthians 9:6**

Rick testified in the program that early in his life, he struggled with giving because he didn't understand that if he gave, God would give back to him. He wasn't very generous and didn't have a lot of blessings in his life. But as he renewed His mind with the Word of God concerning giving (*see* Romans 12:2), the fire of God began to be stirred in his heart in this area of his spiritual walk, and the blessings of God began to ensue.

When you begin to give, it brings fire into your heart. Jesus said that your heart will follow your treasure. Charles Spurgeon said, **"In all my years of service to my Lord, I have discovered a truth that has never failed and has never been compromised. That truth is that it is beyond the realm of possibilities that one has the ability to out give God. Even if I give the whole of my worth to Him, He will find a way to give it back to me even much more than I gave."**

A lot of people quote the following verse of Scripture concerning receiving financial blessing from the Lord. Perhaps you have quoted it too.

> **But my God shall supply all your need according to his riches in glory by Christ Jesus.**
> **Philippians 4:19**

If you study the background and context of this verse, you find that this verse is not actually applicable to everyone. It was written to givers. Paul was originally writing to the Philippians who were believers burning with the fire of God. They deeply desired to give, and their giving released a cycle of blessing and God's abundance in their lives. The fire that inspired them to give ignited *more fire*! And because they had sacrificially given, Paul said to them, in effect, "Because of what you have done, this is what God is going to do for you. He will supply all your need according to His riches in glory by Christ Jesus."

Here is the *Renner Interpretive Version* of Philippians 4:19.

> **But my God will supply all your needs so completely that He will eliminate all your deficiencies. He will meet all your physical, tangible needs until you're so full, you have no more capacity to hold anything else. He will supply all your needs until you're totally filled, packed full, and overflowing to the point of bursting at the seams and spilling over.**

That is what this verse means, and it is a promise made to the generous, not the stingy. The reason why the Philippian congregation was so generous is, their heart was in the work of God, and their treasure followed the course of their heart. Remember Jesus said that where your treasure is, that's where your heart is also (*see* Matthew 6:21). That is a scriptural truth that cannot be denied. And when you give your treasure to God, it literally adds fuel to your spiritual fire. You come alive when you put your finances in the Kingdom of God. If you need to stir your fire, give a sacrificial gift, and you will come *aflame* with the Spirit of God — *it is guaranteed!*

If you have failed in this area of generosity in the past, don't get under condemnation about it because condemnation will never effect change in your life that brings God's blessings. Simply repent, or turn around, and commit to putting finances into the Kingdom of God to demonstrate where your heart is. Talk to the Lord about it, and He will respond to you. Allow Him to ignite His holy fire in your heart as you give that will trigger all kinds of heavenly blessings in your life. This spiritual passion and cycle of blessing is a Bible principle with promise!

STUDY QUESTIONS

> Study to shew thyself approved unto God, a workman that needeth
> not to be ashamed, rightly dividing the word of truth.
> — 2 Timothy 2:15

1. What did Jesus say about giving in the Bible? Why did He devote so much of the Bible to the subject of money?
2. Jesus had a supernatural healing and deliverance ministry — what were some of His other ministries? Go back and study Acts 10:38. What does "doing good" mean here?
3. Generosity flowed through the early New Testament Church. What was their motive, and what were the effects of their giving (*see* Acts 2:42-45)?

PRACTICAL APPLICATION

> But be ye doers of the word, and not hearers only,
> deceiving your own selves.
> — James 1:22

1. When you sow bountifully, you reap bountifully. Consider thoughtfully how you give — specifically with offerings, which is above the normal tithe of ten percent of all your financial increase. When you give from the heart, do you expect to receive something back from God each time? What happened in the Early Church when they gave sacrificially? Evaluate the fire in your heart of generosity toward God.

2. Can you stretch yourself to give sacrificially to the Lord this month or this quarter? If you choose to do so, document the Holy Spirit's response is to your great act of faith.

LESSON 7

TOPIC

Ablaze With Holiness

SCRIPTURES

1. **2 Timothy 1:6** — Wherefore I put thee in remembrance that thou stir up the gift of God, which is in thee by the putting on of my hands.

2. **Romans 1:7** — To all that be in Rome, beloved of God, called to be saints....

3. **1 Corinthians 6:9-11** — Know ye not that the unrighteous shall not inherit the kingdom of God? Be not deceived: neither fornicators, nor idolaters, nor adulterers, nor effeminate, nor abusers of themselves with mankind, nor thieves, nor covetous, nor drunkards, nor revilers, nor extortioners, shall inherit the kingdom of God. And such were some of you....

4. **1 Corinthians 6:11** — ...But ye are washed, but ye are sanctified, but ye are justified in the name of the Lord Jesus, and by the Spirit of our God

5. **1 Thessalonians 4:3,4** — For this is the will of God, even your sanctification,that ye should abstain from fornication: That every one of you should know how to possess his vessel in sanctification and honour.

6. **1 Thessalonians 4:7** — For God hath not called us to uncleanness, but unto holiness.

7. **Romans 6:13 (*NLT*)** — …Give yourselves completely to God since you have been given new life. And use your whole body as a tool to do what is right for the glory of God.

GREEK WORDS

1. "stir up" — **ἀναζωπυρέω** (*anadzopureo*): to be enthusiastic, fervent, passionate, vigorous; to do something wholeheartedly or zealously; to rekindle or to stir back to life again

2. "holy" — **γιος** (*hagios*): separated, consecrated, holy, and sacred — never again to be regarded or used in a common way; anything "holy" is in a category that is separate and sacred from other things

3. "sanctified" — **ἁγιάζω** (*hagiadzo*): from the root word **ἅγιος** (hagios); to set aside; consecrated; made different; made holy

4. "sanctification" — **ἁγιασμός** (*hagiasmos*): from the root word **ἅγιος** (hagios), which is the root word for holy; in this case, it is translated "sanctification," which depicts us living differently from the rest of the world and living in a state of holiness in our daily lives

5. "abstain" — **ἀπέχω** (*apecho*): to abstain; to withdraw from; to stay away from; to put distance between oneself and something else; to deliberately or intentionally refrain from something; to put physical distance between oneself and another person, place, or thing

6. "every one" — **ἕκαστος** (*hekastos*): an all-inclusive term that embraces everyone, with no one excluded

7. "possess" — **κτάομαι** (*ktaomai*): to handle; to gain control over; to manage; to win mastery over

8. "vessel" — **σκεῦος** (*skeuos*): a vessel, container, or utensil; in this case, the human body

9. "sanctification" — **ἁγιασμός** (*hagiasmos*): from the root word **ἅγιος** (hagios), which is the root word for holy; in this case, it is translated "sanctification," which depicts us living differently from the rest of the world and living in a state of holiness in our daily lives

10. "honor" — **τιμή** (*time*): to honor or hold something so valuable that it is precious, prized, cherished, treasured, valuable, and very dear; to assign value to an object or person

SYNOPSIS

When Moses saw God at the mountain in the desert wilderness, he saw a bush that was on fire (*see* Exodus 3:2). The bush was aflame with the glory and fire of God, but it was not being consumed, or burnt. Moses was standing on *holy ground*. In fact, God said to Moses, "...Take off your sandals, for you are standing on holy ground" (v. 5). Right before that, the Lord warned Moses, "Do not come any closer!" That's because God is *a consuming fire*. And He calls for holiness in our life (*see* 1 Peter 1:16). When we throw the fuel of holiness into our spiritual life, it literally sets our heart on fire.

Are you adding holiness to your life? That's a fuel that you need to be ablaze for God for the rest of your days on earth, and that is the topic of this lesson.

Often, we drift in our spiritual life and don't even realize we're drifting. If you look at the early years when you first came to Jesus, when you were really on fire, there were things you did back in those days that fed your spiritual flame. If you feel that your spiritual fire is on a low burn, or you feel like the fire has nearly gone out in your life, this series will help you stir the embers, fan the flames, and burn brightly for Jesus once again.

The emphasis of this lesson:

When many people hear the word "holiness," they immediately think of restrictions and legalism — but that is not what holiness is. Holiness fans the flames of enthusiasm and zeal, ignites the soul, and delights the heart. Holiness brings blessing and *light*. Holiness even gives you a fresh revelation concerning *you* or whatever it is you need to see and receive from God.

The *Holy* Spirit Comes
With Divine Activity and Spiritual Fire!

If you want the fire of God in your life, you need the Holy Spirit to be active in your life. Remember His name is *the Holy* Spirit. It's not just *the Spirit*. He is holy, and the Holy Spirit feels most comfortable in places where there is holiness. So if you're walking in holiness, the Holy Spirit is going to be more visibly active in your life. And where the Holy Spirit is active, *there is fire*.

The Holy Spirit comes with fire. So if you want the fire of God to burn in your life, you have to create an atmosphere where the Holy Spirit is comfortable. God calls us to a life of holiness. Living that lifestyle will bring us divine activity and it will bring us *spiritual fire*.

Our anchor verse is Second Timothy 1:6, in which Paul was writing by the Holy Spirit to Timothy, his son in the faith, whose fire was diminishing to a low burn. Timothy was about to see his fire "evaporated." He was dealing with an onslaught of problems and distractions, and he allowed it to affect his spiritual fire.

What's Possible if You've Allowed Your Fire To Diminish

Has that ever happened to you? You started out aflame with the Spirit in the midst of difficulties, but you began to focus on the problems, trying to resolve them in your own strength or by leaning to your own understanding. Soon you began to feel weak, defeated, and nearly hopeless. You lost your faith, confidence, and momentum because you'd begun to lose your *fire*.

> **Wherefore I put thee in remembrance that thou stir up the gift of God, which is in thee by the putting on of my hands.**
> **2 Timothy 1:6**

Since the Holy Spirit prompted and inspired Paul to write these words of instruction, it tells us that it is very possible to do — we *can* stir up the gift of God in us! But we have to believe it, seize it, and be very intentional to carry it out. We can't wait for someone else to stir us up. *We* have to do it, and we have to do it *on purpose*.

The Greek word translated "stir up" describes *being enthusiastic, fervent, passionate, vigorous, wholehearted, and zealous.* That further tells us that if you're not enthusiastically determined to stir yourself up, it's not going to happen. But if you're zealous about it — if you fervently, passionately, and vigorously put your whole heart into it — you can stir the fire of God in your heart again.

In a Category All by Itself

What is holiness? That's a very important question. In both the *Old Testament* Septuagint and the Greek *New Testament*, the word "holiness," or "holy," come from the word *hagios* in the Greek. So we can easily know what the word "holy" means. It means *to be separated, consecrated, or sacred or set apart*. To walk in holiness means *to never again be regarded or used in a common way.*

Anything holy is in a category that is separate and sacred from other things. It is in a category all by itself. For example, consider the Bible. It is rightly called the *Holy* Bible. Those who translated the Scriptures understood the meaning of the word "holy." The word "Bible" is from the Greek word *biblios*; it simply refers to *a book*. But the Holy Bible is not an ordinary book. A library can be filled with *thousands upon thousands* of books. But in the entire library, there is only one book called the Holy Bible.

Translators attached this word "Holy" to this book's title to make that point that the Bible is in a category of its own. It is separate from all other books. It is *consecrated* and *sacred*. There is not, nor will there ever be, another book like the Bible. The Holy Bible is separate and distinct. *You will never find another book like the Bible!*

Going back to Moses' experience with the burning bush in the wilderness, he'd heard God say, "Moses, you're standing on *holy ground*" (*see* Exodus 3:5). That word "holy" is this word *hagios*, which we know describes *something separate, consecrated, and sacred.* Before God came on the scene, that physical area of land looked no different than surrounding areas. But the area around that bush had been visibly visited and inhabited by God's presence. It became *holy* — *set apart* and *sacred*. The divine presence consecrated it, putting it into a completely separate category. It may have previously looked like other bushes in other mountain deserts. But when the fire of God came, it was no longer like other areas. In that moment, God's divine presence supernaturally separated that mountain and set it apart into a holy category. God's presence set parameters around it, separating it from its surrounding areas. *God's presence changed its status!*

We're Called To Be Set Apart — *Holy*

This New Testament verse describes Christians using that same word *hagios* in the Greek.

> **To all that be in Rome, beloved of God, called to be *saints*....**
> **Romans 1:7**

The word "saints" here was translated from the same Greek word *hagios* — the word "holy" elsewhere in the New Testament. "Called to be saints" means we're called to be *holy*. We're not just Christians or believers — we are *saints*. That means that when God's presence came to us at the time of our new birth, His presence — His Holy Spirit — moved right into us. When we repented and made Jesus Lord and Savior of our life, the divine presence changed our status. We are no longer like others who have not been visited by God's holy presence. We may look like other human beings, but because of the fire of God's presence within us, we are not "normal" at all. We have been set apart and placed into a completely different category — from one of darkness to one of light. We are now "holy ground." The Holy Spirit came into us, and He's comfortable there because our status was changed. We became an environment of holiness, and we are set apart and inhabited by God Himself.

The New Birth — Then What?

Now we have to learn to live like who we really are. We're not who we used to be.

Think about who you used to be before you came to Christ. Many can remember a time when they walked in spiritual darkness. In the following passage, Paul talks about a group of believers whose status had starkly changed when they were inhabited by God's divine presence in the new birth.

> **Know ye not that the unrighteous shall not inherit the kingdom of God? Be not deceived: neither fornicators, nor idolaters, nor adulterers, nor effeminate, nor abusers of themselves with mankind,**
>
> **Nor thieves, nor covetous, nor drunkards, nor revilers, nor extortioners, shall inherit the kingdom of God. And such were some of you....**
>
> **1 Corinthians 6:9-11**

"And such were some of you...." That was a way of saying, "Hey, guys, this is who you used to be — a moral mess!"

The pagans in Corinth were really flawed. Because of the dark moral condition of that entire city, the people who lived there were defective in character in almost every way. Before they were saved, they were fornicators, idolaters, adulterers, effeminate, abusers of themselves with mankind, thieves, covetous, drunkards, revilers, and extortioners.

But look at what Paul said after he said, "That used to be *you!*"

> **...But ye are washed, but ye are sanctified, but ye are justified in the name of the Lord Jesus, and by the Spirit of our God.**
> **1 Corinthians 6:11**

First Paul rehearsed the darkness these Corinthian believers had been delivered from. Then he said, *"But you are now washed."*

Thank God, we are not who we used to be! When the blood of Jesus touched us, we were *washed.* This word "washed" describes a thorough cleansing at a specific moment in your past that occurred the moment you repented — turned to Christ — and came to Him, making Him the Lord of your life.

In the new birth, the Holy Spirit came into you to abide — inside you where you had been washed clean. Your past is gone. But that's not all that happened. Paul said, "You were washed and *sanctified.*" The divine presence came to indwell you, setting you apart as *separate* and *holy.*

That's what that word "sanctified" means. It's from the Greek word *hagiadzo,* a form of *hagios.* The meaning is the same: *to set aside, consecrate, or make sacred.* Just as the Holy Bible is set apart from other books, and just as the burning bush was set apart from all bushes, when the Holy Spirit came to live inside those Corinthian believers in the new birth, they were no longer like other Corinthians in their city. Their status was changed, and they became *hagios* — sanctified and set aside. And the same is true of you.

J. I. Packard said, **"Holiness is in fact commanded: God wills it, Christ requires it, and all the Scriptures — the law, the gospel, the prophets, the wisdom writings, the epistles, the history books that tell of judgments past and the book of Revelation that tells of judgment to come — call for it."**

Fulfilling God's Will for Your Life

Believers are called to holiness because that's who they are. They are set apart as holy, so it is inappropriate to behave in unholy ways. Unholy is who we used to be, but we were "washed and sanctified." We are no longer the same.

> **For this is the will of God, even your sanctification, that ye should abstain from fornication.**
> **1 Thessalonians 4:3**

Rick related on the program that the number-one question people write to him about is the will and plan of God for their life. The will of God can be found in the Word of God. First Thessalonians 4:3 lets you know that the will of God for your life is "your sanctification, that you should abstain from fornication."

Again, "sanctification" is a form of the Greek word *hagios*. It depicts us living differently from the rest of the world and living in a state of holiness in our daily lives. Our status has been changed; we're not who we used to be. Who we were is not who we are. When the Holy Spirit came into us, that divine act separated us from our past. We were washed in the blood of Jesus, and we were sanctified. Parameters were placed around us in the spirit, and God said, "This is holy ground."

First Thessalonians 4:3 goes on to say, "…That ye should abstain from fornication." That means that since your status has changed, you shouldn't live like you once did. That's not legalism; that is simply living up to your new status.

We're not to live according to who we used to be, but according to who we are. God made us holy; therefore we're to live a sanctified, holy life. We're to abstain from fornication — from who we used to be.

The word "abstain" is the Greek word *apecho*, and it means *to withdraw from; to stay away from; to put distance between oneself and something else; to deliberately or intentionally refrain from something; or to put physical distance between oneself and another person, place, or thing.*

In fact, this Bible command could be translated like this: "Put space between you and any kind of temptation you're facing. You must build a barrier between yourself and the temptations so that it is impossible for you to cross the barrier and do what is inappropriate for a holy person to do."

As a believer, you're not walking in holiness to *become* holy; you're walking in holiness because you *are* holy. That's who you are. Unholiness is simply inappropriate for your new status. This is really what this Scripture is commanding us: *Live up to your new status, your new life in Christ!*

> **That every one of you should know how to possess his vessel in sanctification and honour.**
>
> **1 Thessalonians 4:4**

When Paul said "every one," he used the Greek word *hekastos*, an all-inclusive term that embraces everyone with no one excluded. So this verse applies to every single believer in Christ with no exclusions.

Every Christian should know how to possess his vessel in sanctification and honor. The word "possess" is from the Greek word that means *to handle; to gain control over; to manage;* or *to win mastery over.* The word "vessel" is translated from a Greek word that describes a *vessel* or *container,* but in this case, it's talking about *the human body.* This verse is really talking about body management. Each believer needs to know how to manage himself and his life. God has called us to sanctification and honor.

We know the word "sanctification" is from a form of the word *hagios* and means *to be separate.* But what about "honor"? It's from the Greek word that means to hold something so valuable that it is *precious, prized, cherished, treasured, valuable, and very dear.* It means *to assign value to an object or to a person.*

Your body is the temple of the Holy Spirit (1 Corinthians 16:9)! You are precious, and your body is precious. So treat your body like it is the temple of the Holy Spirit because it is. Live up to your new status in Christ. There's a blessing in that. The fire of God will come — fire that provides warmth, cleansing, power, and light. You'll even sleep better because you'll know you're living in line with the divine presence in your life and your new status.

> **For God hath not called us unto uncleanness, but unto holiness.**
>
> **1 Thessalonians 4:7**

God has called us to live separate, consecrated lives and to be different. He has called us to live as if we are sacred — *because we are.* We are sacred, holy ground where God's presence dwells.

...Give yourselves completely to God, for you were dead, but now you have new life. (And) So use your whole body as an instrument (tool) to do what is right for the glory of God.
Romans 6:13

Billy Graham made the following statement: "We have largely lost sight of the holiness and purity of God today. This is one reason why we tolerate sin so easily." God is holy, and He has made us holy. He visited us with His divine presence and changed our status. A sinner is who we used to be — not who we are today. God separated us for Him — He put parameters around us. He put barriers around us, saying, "They are Mine!" With this awareness of God's holiness and what He has made us, we should not tolerate sin in our life.

When you live like this, the activity of the Holy Spirit becomes abundant in your life, and it sets your heart aflame. The fire of God will burn in your life like an inferno for years and years to come.

STUDY QUESTIONS

Study to shew thyself approved unto God, a workman that needeth not to be ashamed, rightly dividing the word of truth.
— 2 Timothy 2:15

1. What does the Greek word *hagios* mean? What did it mean when God called the ground Moses stood on "holy ground"? What effect did it have on that particular mountain?
2. How do we give ourselves completely to God? Is it a one-time event? What is the process? What happened during the new birth that enables us to live holy lives?

PRACTICAL APPLICATION

But be ye doers of the word, and not hearers only, deceiving your own selves.
— James 1:22

1. In what ways have you separated yourself unto holiness since you came to Christ? Are there actions you can take today that will give God greater opportunity to help you manage your body and your life?

2. What do you abstain from now that you didn't when you were a new believer? What might you have to lay down now that is a hindrance, that may be preventing the Holy Spirit from fully operating in your life? Have you rigorously kept a guard over your lips and heart or have you allowed yourself to become polluted by the world? What made you aware of that? Be accountable by writing it down and sharing it with a safe, seasoned person. Ask the Lord to help you and strengthen you to maintain your offensive, dominant leadership position in living a holy life for Him.

3. Do you carefully choose your friends? Did you ask the Lord who He wants you to be friends with? We should not act like the world as we continue growing in our Christian walk — it is a blessing to have a band of believers help us walk the narrow path of holiness. Do you have friends who help you live the way the Bible says to live — who love you and your divine destiny and who can speak into your life?

LESSON 8

TOPIC
Ablaze With Humility

SCRIPTURES

1. **2 Timothy 1:6** — Wherefore I put thee in remembrance that thou stir up the gift of God, which is in thee by the putting on of my hands.

2. **James 4:6** — ...God resisteth the proud....

3. **Romans 12:3 (*AMPC*)** — For by the grace (unmerited favor of God) given to me I warn everyone among you not to estimate and think of himself more highly than he ought [not to have an exaggerated opinion of his own importance], but to rate his ability with sober judgment, each according to the degree of faith apportioned by God to him.

4. **Psalm 24:18** — The Lord is nigh unto them that are of a broken heart; and saveth such as be of a contrite spirit.

5. **Psalm 51:17** — The sacrifices of God are a broken spirit: a broken and contrite heart, O God, thou wilt not despise.

6. **Isaiah 57:15** — For thus saith the high and lofty One that inhabiteth eternity, whose name is Holy; I dwell in the high and holy place, with him also that is of a contrite and humble spirit, to revive the spirit of the humble, and to revive the heart of the contrite ones

7. **Isaiah 66:2** — For all those things hath mine hand made, and all those things have been, saith the Lord: but to this man will I look, even to him that is poor and of a contrite spirit, and trembleth at my word.

GREEK WORDS

1. "resisteth" — ἀντιτάσσω (*antitasso*): a military term that depicts the orderly arrangement of troops to successively wage combat against the non-compliant; it is a deliberate, premeditated arrangement of military might to crush an enemy; a well-planned, prepared resistance; to stand against; to set one's self against; to resist

2. "proud" — ὑπερήφανος (*huperephanos*), from ὑπερ (*huper*) and φανος (*phanos*): the word ὑπερ (*huper*) depicts something that is above or superior, and φανος (*phanos*) means to be manifested; when compounded, it paints a picture of a person who sees himself above the rest of the crowd; one who has an arrogant, haughty, high-and-mighty, and insolent attitude; one who thinks he is intellectually advantaged above others

3. "humble" — ταπεινός (*tapeinos*): one who has become humble; to reduce one's self-importance; to make small; to minimize oneself; to be willing to stoop to any measure that is needed

4. "more highly" — ὑπερφρονέω (*huperphroneo*), a compound of ὑπέρ (*huper*) and φρονέω (*phroneo*): the word ὑπέρ (*huper*) means over, above, or beyond; the word φρονέω (*phroneo*) means to think; to think of oneself more highly than he ought to think; to have an exaggerated opinion of one's own importance

5. "grace" — χάρις (*charis*): ancient Greece, a touch of the gods resulting in favor or grace; an empowering touch; an empowering presence, always demonstrating itself with a visible manifestation; a power that changes individuals; a power that enables one to do what he previously could not do

SYNOPSIS

In this series, we're talking about spiritual fire and how to stay on fire for the Lord for years to come as you run your spiritual race. Do you know how to stir up the fire in your heart? To keep the fire burning, you need the right fuel.

So far, we have examined six other fuels you need to stir up the fire in your heart: the Word of God, prayer, the Holy Spirit, worship, generosity, and holiness. Another fuel we need to add to stay ablaze for God is *humility*.

Emphasis of this lesson:

The Bible says, "God resisteth the proud, and giveth grace to the humble" (James 4:6). When people are walking in biblical humility, God is attracted to that like metal to a magnet! He comes to those people and sets their hearts *ablaze*.

Humility is a fuel to add to the fire of one's heart to keep it ablaze. Biblical humility is not about putting oneself down or berating oneself — that's a work of the flesh. Biblical humility is an attitude of the heart that trusts God, depends on God, and *pleases* God.

As we've seen, even if your fire is burning low, you can do something intentionally to get it set ablaze again. Paul wrote to Timothy, "Wherefore I put thee in remembrance that thou stir up the gift of God, which is in thee by the putting on of my hands" (2 Timothy 1:6). According to this verse, it's up to us to stir up the gift of God in us — to throw another log on the flame so we can begin burning again for Him.

Pride Is a Fire-Killer and Can Be Fatal to Our Spiritual Life

Before looking at humility, we must know this: Pride is fatal. Unhealthy pride is so fatal that we must learn how to identify and eliminate it; we must uproot it from our lives. If an unhealthy pride is working in us, God Himself will stand against us!

Pride is an equal-opportunity eliminator! Every person who operates in pride is eventually eliminated. Remember that Lucifer was eliminated due to his pride. In the Old Testament case of Absalom, he was eliminated because of his pride. And Judas Iscariot was eliminated as well.

Rick found out this truth early in his own life when he thought he was better than the pastor he was serving. He judged and condemned him, a man who had been in the ministry more than 40 years. As a young man in his 20s, Rick thought he was greater and more anointed than his mentor. Yet when Rick was out of the picture, his pastor was still in his pulpit and his ministry continued. But pride had eliminated Rick, which was the devil's purpose. The devil's goal is to tempt people to get into pride because if they do, they will be removed from the scene. Pride will quench the fire of God burning in their heart. Unhealthy pride is so bad that James 4:6 says, "…God *resisteth* the proud…."

God Resists the Proud

In James 4:6, God was speaking to believers. It says, "…God resisteth the proud, but giveth grace unto the humble." Biblical humility is powerful because God will give power to the person who is humble. What does the word "humble" mean? The Greek word for humble is *tapeinos*, describing *one who has become humbled*. It depicts one formally operating in pride, but through some act of God or some change of behavior or repentance, one has become humbled. It also means *to reduce one's self-importance; to make small; to minimize oneself;* or *to be willing to stoop to any measure that is needed*. So this word portrays a person who was once arrogant, but then has become humbled.

Romans 12:3 (*AMPC*) says, "For by the grace (unmerited favor of God) given to me I warn everyone among you not to estimate and think of himself more highly than he ought…." Those words "more highly" are *very* important. In this particular verse, the word used is a Greek word, *huperephanos*, which is a compound of two words, *huper*, which means *above* or *something superior*, and *phreno*, a Greek word meaning *to think*. When compounded to form the word *huperephanos*, it means *to think of oneself more highly than he ought to think* or *to have an exaggerated opinion of one's own importance*.

When someone has a bloated or inflated opinion of himself, he sees himself as being "high and mighty." He might think he's better or more anointed than his employer, pastor, etc. His opinion of himself has gone to his head. It is unhealthy pride.

Scripture warns us that when we are found operating in such pride, we will be eliminated in the situations and circumstances of life. We must identify and uproot pride! If unhealthy pride is *not* repented of, a moment will come when God will get involved to resist it. The best thing we can do is to stop pride before it starts, because if God Almighty is resisting us, we must throw in the towel, surrender, and repent. Continuing is useless. We are on hold until we get rid of pride!

Humility is the necessary fuel to inject into our spiritual flame because God gives grace to the humble. Many don't understand the meaning of the word "humble." They think it means to be wishy-washy. No, the humble receive God's grace, power, and *fire*.

The word "humility" comes from the Greek word *tapeinos* and describes one who has been humbled. A person in this humble condition has reduced one's self-importance. To be humble means to make small, to minimize oneself, or to be willing to stoop to any measure that is needed. By definition, humility portrays someone who was once arrogant, but now has become humbled. He has come down from his haughty position to conform to a new behavior that God expects of him. To be humble, one has a modest view of himself as opposed to an exaggerated view.

James 4:6 says that God gives grace to the humble. The Greek word for "graces is *charis*. It describes "a touch of the gods" that resulted in favor or grace; an empowering touch or presence; a demonstration with a visible manifestation. It is a power that changes a person, a power than enables him to do what he previously could not do on his own.

God Gets Involved With Biblical Humility

A person who possesses biblical humility makes room for God to get involved in his life. God gives grace and provides power and whatever is needed to change that person. Like metal drawn to a magnet, God comes on the scene to a person who is humble and causes the fire of the Spirit to burn brightly in that individual's life.

Scripture describes biblical humility in Psalm 34:18: "The Lord is nigh unto them that are of a broken heart; and saveth such as be of a contrite spirit." Psalm 51:17 says, "The sacrifices of God are a broken spirit: a broken and a contrite heart, O God, thou wilt not despise."

Isaiah 66:2 says, "For all those things hath mine hand made, and all those things have been, saith the Lord: but to this man will I look, even to him that is poor and of a contrite spirit, and trembleth at my word."

God *does* resist the proud, but He will give *grace* to the humble. Pride will eliminate you, but humility will promote you. And to have the fire of God working in one's life, he must have humility. This is the fuel a believer needs to add to keep his spiritual fire burning strong for a long, long time to come. God will stand against the proud person, but He will give grace, a supernatural touch and everything needed, to anyone who humbles himself.

Humility attracts the presence of God. A humble attitude invites Him on the scene, and God responds. And when God manifests Himself, fire is there, power is present, and everything that is necessary for that believer comes.

Humility may seem weak to those who are walking after the flesh, but God uses it to cause the humble believer to become a spiritual inferno for Him. Humility is truly a fuel that feeds the fire of the heart for Jesus.

STUDY QUESTIONS

Study to shew thyself approved unto God, a workman that needeth not to be ashamed, rightly dividing the word of truth.
— 2 Timothy 2:15

1. What is biblical humility? What does it mean when it says God gives grace to the humble? Can you describe the good type of promotion that comes to the humble at heart?

2. What is unhealthy pride? Why is it so lethal to the plans and purposes of God in a person's life? Why is it called the equal-opportunity eliminator? List others from the Bible besides those mentioned in this lesson, who were eliminated by their pride against God.

PRACTICAL APPLICATION

But be ye doers of the word, and not hearers only, deceiving your own selves.
—James 1:22

1. Can you recall a time when you were humbled but didn't see your wrongdoing until much later? What did it take for you "see" with the eyes of biblical humility? Pride is deceptive and subtle. Did you see the warnings?

2. The Word says God is close to those with a broken spirit and a contrite heart. How did the Lord help you when you were broken-hearted? Recall what He did and how He came to you because you humbly looked to Him.

3. What do you do to remain humble in your daily walk with God? How do you stay accountable to God? What do you do to check up on yourself to ensure that you're not ensnared by pride?

TOPIC

Ablaze With the Fear of the Lord

SCRIPTURES

1. **2 Timothy 1:6** — Wherefore I put thee in remembrance that thou stir up the gift of God, which is in thee by the putting on of my hands.

2. **Ecclesiastes 12:13** — Let us hear the conclusion of the whole matter: Fear God, and keep his commandments: for this is the whole duty of man. For God shall bring every work into judgment, with every secret thing, whether it be good, or whether it be evil.

3. **Psalm 31:19** — Oh how great is thy goodness, which thou hast laid up for them that fear thee....

4. **Psalm 112:1** — Those who **fear the Lord will be greatly blessed.**

5. **Psalm 115:11** — Those who fear the Lord will find Him to be their help and shield to protect them in times of trouble.

6. **Proverbs 14:26,27** — Those who fear the Lord will have confidence, find a place of refuge, and they will have a fountain of life.

7. **Proverbs 22:4** — Those who fear the Lord will experience **riches, honor, and life**

8. **Psalm 147:10,11** — His delight is not in the strength of the horse, nor his pleasure in the legs of a man, but the Lord takes pleasure in those who fear him, in those who hope in his steadfast love.

9. **1 Peter 1:15-17** — But as he which hath called you is holy, so be ye holy in all manner of conversation; Because it is written, Be ye holy;

for I am holy. And if ye call on the Father, who without respect of persons judgeth according to every man's work, pass the time of your sojourning here in fear....

10. **Psalm 34:11** — Come, ye children, hearken unto me: I will teach you the fear of the Lord.

11. **Proverbs 9:10** — The fear of the Lord is the beginning of wisdom: and the knowledge of the holy is understanding.

12. **Psalm 111:10** — The fear of the Lord is the beginning of wisdom: a good understanding have all they that do his commandments: his praise endureth forever.

13. **Proverbs 1:7** — The fear of the Lord is the beginning of knowledge: but fools despise wisdom and instruction.

14. **Acts 2:42,43** — And they continued steadfastly in the apostles' doctrine and fellowship, and in breaking of bread, and in prayers. And fear came upon every soul: and many wonders and signs were done by the apostles.

15. **Acts 5:1** — But a certain man named Ananias, with Sapphira his wife, sold a possession, and kept back part of the price, his wife also being privy to it, and brought a certain part, and laid it at the apostles' feet.

16. **Acts 5:3,4** — …Why hath Satan filled thine heart to lie to the Holy Ghost, and to keep back part of the price of the land? While it remained, was it not thine own? And after it was sold, was it not in thine own power? Why hast thou conceived this thing in thine heart? Thou hast not lied unto men, but unto God.

17. **Acts 5:5-6** — And Ananias hearing these words fell down, and gave up the ghost: and great fear came on all them that heard these things. And the young men arose, wound him up, and carried him out, and buried him.

18. **Acts 5:7** — And it was about the space of three hours after, when his wife, not knowing what was done, came in. And Peter answered unto her, Tell me whether ye sold the land for so much? And she said, Yea, for so much.

19. **Acts 5:9** — Then Peter said unto her, How is it that ye have agree together to tempt the Spirit of the Lord? Behold, the feet of them which have buried thy husband are at the door, and shall carry thee out.

20. **Acts 5:10** — Then fell she down straightway at his feet, and yielded up the ghost: and the young men came in, and found her dead, and carrying her forth, buried her by her husband.

21. **Acts 5:11** — And great fear came upon all the church, and upon as many as heard these things

22. **Acts 5:12** — ...Many signs and wonders wrought among the people....

23. **Acts 5:16** — ...They brought forth the sick into the streets and laid them on beds and couches, that at the least the shadow of Peter passing by might overshadow some of them. There came also a multitude out of the cities round about unto Jerusalem, bringing sick folks, and them which were vexed with unclean spirits: and they were healed every one.

GREEK WORDS

1. "stir up" — ἀναζωπυρέω (*anadzopureo*): to be enthusiastic, fervent, passionate, vigorous; to do something wholeheartedly or zealously; to rekindle or to stir back to life again

2. "conversation" — ναστροφή (*anastrophe*): depicts lifestyle; a person's rising up and sitting down; pictures how a person conducts life and how he behaves in every situation; a person's total conduct and lifestyle — his rising up, sitting down, etc.

SYNOPSIS

We have covered the different types of fuel needed to keep the fire of God burning in one's heart so that he or she can stay ablaze with the Holy Ghost for years and years to come. We talked about the need to have the Word of God in our lives, prayer in our lives, the work of the Holy Spirit active in our lives, and worship, generosity, holiness, and humility — because they all attract the presence of God. *They are fire-igniters!* Another fuel needed to stay on fire for the Lord is *the fear of the Lord.*

The emphasis of this lesson:

We must maintain a healthy fear of the Lord. There is no need for confusion about what the fear of the Lord is and how we apply to our lives. Where there is an active fear of the Lord, there is spiritual fire and spiritual power. Fearing the Lord is so important that we are told

300 times in the Bible that we need to have healthy fear of the Lord. And there are promises that belong to those who fear God. They will be greatly blessed. They will find Him to be their help and shield in times of trouble. They will have confidence, a place of refuge, and a fountain of life. Those who fear the Lord will experience riches, honor, and long life. Fearing God is the duty of man!

Fearing God Is Man's Duty

Our anchor text is Second Timothy 1:6: "Wherefore I put thee in remembrance that thou stir up the gift of God, which is in thee by the putting on of my hands." To stir up what was placed inside us by God is to bring the fire of the Holy Spirit back to life in our life again. To do that, we need to add the fuels that help us refire the power of God in our heart.

Ecclesiastes 12:13,14 says, "Let us hear the conclusion of the whole matter: Fear God, and keep his commandments: for this is the whole duty of man. For God shall bring every work into judgement, with every secret thing, whether it be good, or whether it be evil."

This passage tells us that it is the duty of every one of us to fear the Lord. In fact, in Scripture, we are commanded 300 times to have a fear of the Lord. So we *must* have a healthy fear of God. To do that, we first need to understand what it means to fear the Lord.

Reverentially fearing the Lord is a good, healthy thing. The psalmist said in Psalm 31:19, "Oh how great is thy goodness, which thou has laid up for them that fear thee…." The promise of this verse belongs to those who fear the Lord. Great goodness is laid up for those who fear the Lord.

Psalm 147:10,11 says, "He delighteth not in the strength of the horse: he taketh not pleasure in the legs of the man. The Lord takes pleasure in them that fear him, in those who hope in His mercy." According to this verse, God takes pleasure in those that fear Him.

J. Oswald Sanders said, **"The remarkable thing about God is that when you fear God, you fear nothing else; whereas, if you do not fear God you fear everything else."** And Charles Spurgeon said, **"He who fears God has nothing else to fear."**

What Is the Fear of the Lord?

Many people struggle with the fear of the Lord because they are confused about healthy, reverential fear and respect for someone versus tormenting fear that one might feel when they are in terrible, imminent danger. Since pastors want their people to draw near to the Lord instead of running from Him in fear, many of them and other spiritual leaders as well have changed "*fear* of the Lord" to "*respect* for the Lord." Respect is certainly a part of the fear of the Lord, but just "respect" doesn't do the meaning of *the fear of the Lord* justice. It simply does not embrace and encompass the whole meaning.

Familiarity Breeds Sin

Therefore, in our attempt to make God approachable, people have gone in an opposite direction of the healthy fear of the Lord. They have become very casual with God, and they have lost their fear of Him. By making God too approachable — based on their own methods of approaching Him versus the biblically prescribed way — people, even believers, have begun to live casually. Their spiritual sight has been eclipsed, and they no longer see God as both loving *and* holy. They live in sin without conviction or concern about ramifications or retribution. They put too much emphasis on the mercy of God and have forgotten that they belong to God and are accountable to Him for their life.

When people lose their fear of the Lord, the power of God begins to diminish; the fire of the Holy Spirit dwindles as well. But where there is an active fear of the Lord, the power of God is there, the fire of God is there.

Peter emphasizes the importance of this when he wrote:

> **But as he, which hath called you, is holy, so be ye holy in all manner of conversation; Because it is written, Be ye holy; for I am holy. And if you call on the Father, who without respect of persons judgeth according to every man's work, pass the time of your sojourning here in fear.**
>
> **1 Peter 1:15-17**

Here, the word "conversation" is not talking about talking. It is from the Greek word *anastrophe*, and it depicts *lifestyle* or *whole manner of lifestyle*

— a person's rising up and sitting down; coming in and going out — in other words, how he conducts his total lifestyle.

Love Is of God — and So Is His Holy Fear

Our entire life should reflect holiness. The end of the verse says, "…Pass the time of your sojourning here in fear." The word "fear" is the Greek word *phobos*, which really is the word for *fear*. In essence, Peter was saying if we call on God as our Heavenly Father, that does not exempt us from consequences. Life is not a game. We need to be very serious and sober about the way we live our lives.

In Psalm 34:11, we find we can be *taught* the fear of the Lord, "Come, ye children, hearken unto me: I will teach you the fear of the Lord." So we must be taught what the fear of the Lord is. That's the topic of this lesson.

People get confused about this subject and often ask about First John 4:18, which says, "…Perfect love casteth out fear.…" God is love (*see* 1 John 4:8). Since that God-kind of love is of God, *the reverential fear of God is of God too.* And that personal knowledge of His perfect love — *and* of His perfect, reverential fear — casts out tormenting, torturing fear.

Choices in Life Have Consequences

There's no question about it: Life has consequences. In the program, Rick used the natural characteristics of electricity to give an example of how we should respect and handle the things of God. If we fear God according to His Word, we receive good, positive, blessed outcomes. He promises it in Scripture! If we mishandle our treatment of Him, we are faced with reaping the consequences of that choice.

When used properly and respectfully, electricity brings blessing. But that same electricity that can be a blessing can also bring negative consequences if it is mishandled. The problem is not with the electricity: Electricity can be a tremendous blessing or it can bring serious, negative consequences. It simply depends on the person who is handling it. Therefore, the outcome lies with the *handler* of electricity, not the electricity itself.

Rick recalled that when he was a young boy, he watched his dad as he worked on the attic fan. His father handled the electricity wrongly, and the shock of it blew him all the way across the attic. Trembling and with his eyebrows seared, Rick's dad had been "fried" by that electricity — he experienced a negative outcome — because it was handled wrong. He mishandled it, and there was a consequence!

Handling Holy Things

God's power can bring healing and deliverance. God's power can bring us benefits and blessings. But if we mishandle it, it can produce negative results. The problem lies not with God, but with our *"handling"* of God. If we violate spiritual principles, there are negative consequences. We must have very healthy respect for God and a reverential fear of mishandling holy things.

Many wonder why they haven't gone further in their spiritual walk than they've gone. Could it be that they have missed building their life on some very foundational truths, such as the fear of the Lord? The fear of the Lord is *foundational* to our life, meaning the fear of the Lord comes first, and everything else is built on the foundation of that.

Consider the following two passages from the book of Proverbs. They are two among many in this book of the Bible.

The fear of the Lord is the beginning of wisdom….
Proverbs 9:10

The fear of the Lord is the beginning of knowledge….
Proverbs 1:7

We see that we have no need to be afraid of electricity if we handle it correctly. Similarly, we have no reason to ever be afraid of God if we deal with Him reverentially and respectfully. God's power is present to be a blessing, but if we do wrong, there will be a negative consequence. The spiritual realm has laws, and when those laws are broken, negative consequences result. And Christians are not exempt from these laws.

A. W. Tozer said, **"When men no longer fear God, they transgress His laws without hesitation. The fear of consequences is no deterrent when the fear of God is gone."** Yet these same people don't understand that when they transgress the laws of God, there *are* negative consequences. *Just because they have no concern about consequences doesn't mean those consequences won't happen!*

But when we have a fear of God and understand that violating spiritual principles carries negative consequences, we live our lives more respectfully. We live more responsibly because we understand there are consequences if we do what is wrong.

Motives Reveal True Character and Show Whether We Really Fear the Lord

The book of Acts illustrates the motives of two people who knowingly mishandled the power of God.

In Acts 4, we can read that a man named Joses sold a large piece of land he owned and brought the money and laid it at the apostles' feet. The people were so overwhelmed by his generous gift that they asked to him to change his name to Barnabas, which means "encourager" or "son of encouragement." He became sort of a "celebrity" because of his sacrificial gift. His popularity among the people certainly grew.

Another man and woman in the church in Jerusalem, Ananias and Sapphira, due to their impure motives, wanted this "celebrity" status in the church as well. When they saw Joses suddenly become so popular because of his heartfelt sacrificial gift, they made a deal between themselves. Ananias and Sapphira said, essentially, "Let's do the same thing and we, too, will become celebrities."

> **But a certain man named Ananias, with Sapphira his wife, sold a possession,** *and kept back part of the price*, **his wife also being privy to it, and brought a certain part, and laid it at the apostles' feet.**
>
> **Acts 5:1**

There was nothing wrong with this couple selling land and keeping back a part of the profit while giving the rest to the church. It was their land; they didn't *have* to give the whole amount. But they presented an inaccurate picture — that was the problem. They said they'd sold the land and were giving the entire amount — all their profit — to the Lord. But they had conspired between themselves to keep back part of it for themselves while giving everyone the impression that they were doing what Barnabas had done so they could gain his status in the eyes of the people.

That was a serious mishandling of the fear of the Lord and the power of God. In their lack of His holy fear, they lost sight of the fact that we all live in the eyesight of God. This couple had impure motives and were insincere in their dealings.

Peter perceived all of this by the power of the Holy Spirit.

> **…Peter said, Ananias, why hath Satan filled thine heart to lie to the Holy Ghost, and to keep back part of the price of the land?**
>
> **Whiles it remained, was it not thine own power? Why hast thou conceived this thing in thine heart? thou hast not lied unto men, but unto God.**
>
> **And Ananias hearing these words fell down, and gave up the ghost: and great fear came on all them that heard these things.**
> **Acts 5:3-5**

Notice it doesn't say that "great respect" came on all who heard — it says that "great *fear*" came upon them. When Ananias fell dead, people were shaken and stunned. They understood, *Wow. We don't lie to the Holy Ghost. We do not deal impurely with the things of God and the power of God. Men may be deceived by our hidden motives, but God is neither deceived, nor mocked.*

Of course, we know that when Ananias' wife Sapphira entered and said exactly the same thing as her husband, not knowing what had befallen him, she experienced the same consequence. This couple crossed a barrier they never should have crossed. They mishandled the power of God, and the result was not healing, deliverance, and blessing. The result was negative; they had forsaken the fear of the Lord.

What is amazing to note is that the same power, in the same chapter in the book of Acts, had been healing the sick, raising the dead, casting out demons, and so on. When handled correctly, the power of God brought great blessing to the Church and to the people. But when handled incorrectly, the outcome was very different.

The lesson in the book of Acts is that when there is a healthy fear of the Lord, there is always an influx of divine power — spiritual fire. And today we as believers need to cultivate and maintain a healthy, reverential respect and fear of God in our life.

Remember we are commanded 300 times in Scripture to have this kind of reverential fear of the Lord. We never have to be afraid in a wrong way of our loving heavenly Father. But He is a holy God, who teaches us in

His Word how to obey Him, enjoy Him, and to stay on fire and zealous for spiritual things. Aligning ourselves with Him and His Word on these matters will bring us blessing and spiritual fervency and fire for years and years to come.

STUDY QUESTIONS

Study to shew thyself approved unto God, a workman that needeth not to be ashamed, rightly dividing the word of truth.
— 2 Timothy 2:15

1. Proverbs 9:10 tells us that the fear of the Lord is the beginning of wisdom. What are some of the many blessings, noted in Scripture, that we receive when we walk in the reverential fear of God?

2. Name a few things that the power of God does. For example, what are some of the blessings? What in Scripture are some of the consequences of the *improper* handling of His power due to a wrong, sinful, casual attitude toward Him?

3. Ananias and Sapphira brought judgment upon themselves. What did they do to cause this? Why did God consider it blasphemous? What do their actions show us about the importance of the reverential fear of the Lord?

PRACTICAL APPLICATION

But be ye doers of the word, and not hearers only, deceiving your own selves.
— James 1:22

1. The apostles changed Joses name to Barnabas ("encourager") when he gave sacrificially to the work of the ministry from his heart. Reflect on similar instances in which God gave *you* seed to sow into His Kingdom, and you acted on that from your heart, with a right motive.

2. Have you ever become conscious by the power of the Holy Spirit of a time you did something with a dishonest, impure motive? Did you quickly repent and turn from that action? The Holy Spirit is faithful to lovingly correct and reprove us when we miss it. Write about the importance of staying in His fear and in tune with Him so we can sensitively and responsibly respond to Him when He deals with us.

TOPIC
Ablaze With Souls

SCRIPTURES

1. **2 Timothy 1:6** — Wherefore I put thee in remembrance that thou stir up the gift of God, which is in thee by the putting on of my hands.

2. **Matthew 28:18-20** — All power is given unto me in heaven and in earth Go ye therefore, and teach all nations, baptizing them in the name of the Father, and of the Son, and of the Holy Ghost: Teaching them to observe all things whatsoever I have commanded you: and, lo, I am with you always, even unto the end of the world. Amen.

3. **Matthew 28:20** — ...And, lo, I am with you always, even unto the end of the world. Amen.

GREEK WORDS

1. "stir up" — ἀναζωπυρέω (*anadzopureo*): to be enthusiastic, fervent, passionate, vigorous; to do something wholeheartedly or zealously; to rekindle or to stir back to life again

SYNOPSIS

God wants us to stay on fire for Him continually. If we have lost the fire of God, we must stir up the fire by adding the necessary fuels to keep ourselves ablaze. This lesson covers the fuel of *having a passion for souls*. We need this fuel to add to our fire and set it ablaze as we run our earthly race.

Emphasis of this lesson:

The Early Church was ablaze, a spiritual inferno, for Jesus. They were also ablaze with a passion for souls because they adhered to the Great Commission given to them by Christ Himself. Today, if we will go into all the world — both our nearby world and the ends of the earth — to win souls, God will regularly release His awesome power and presence in our lives.

Our foundational verse is Second Timothy 1:6: "Wherefore I put thee in remembrance that thou stir up the gift of God, which is in thee by the putting on of my hands."

In review, "stir up" is the Greek word *anadzopureo*, a compound of three words: *ana*, *zao*, and *pur*. The word *ana* means *to repeat something or to do something again*. The word *zao* means *to be lively or full of life*. And the word *pur* is the word *fire*. Compounded, this word *anadzopureo* means *to do whatever one has to do to put life back into his fire again*.

There are intentional things we can do to stir up the gift of God within us, to stir the fire back into full flame again. And one intentional thing we can do to add fuel to our spiritual fire is to cultivate and maintain a passion for souls.

In Matthew 28, Jesus makes the following astounding promise.

> **...All power is given unto me in heaven and in earth. Go ye therefore, and teach all nations, baptizing them in the name of the Father, and of the Son, and of the Holy Ghost: Teaching them to observe all things whatsoever I have commanded you: and, lo, I am with you always, even unto the end of the world. Amen.**
>
> **Matthew 28:18-20**

Essentially, if we go as commanded *and keep going*, we will regularly release God's power and presence in our lives.

This passage is not describing a one-time missions trip or occasionally sharing Christ with someone. It is describing a lifestyle. Christ commands that we go *and keep going*. He is instructing us to "go" as a lifestyle to reach the unsaved with the Gospel.

When we come to verse 20, Jesus makes an astounding promise. He says, "...And, lo, I am with you always, even unto the end of the world. Amen." The word "lo" in Greek is so strong and difficult to translate, but it means, "And, wow — this is just amazing — I will ever be with you." The "lo" belongs to those who "go"!

Obeying this passage and maintaining a passion for reaching the lost ensures God's promise of our experiencing His amazing presence and power. That means if we want to experience this regularly, we're going to have to regularly stir up the fire within us with this fuel of a passion for souls.

To regularly experience the power of God, we'll have to engage regularly in what triggers that power. This is the promise of the Great Commission. The manifested presence of God will be demonstrated in the life of any believer, church or ministry organization that will "go" with the gospel.

The Fire Inside an Evangelizing Church

In the program, Rick recounts a serious miscalculation by the minister in a church he attended as a young man. That church was *filled* with the power of God as leadership encouraged the small congregation to regularly go with the Gospel to the unsaved. They went out on the streets, had a coffee-house ministry, knocked on doors, handed out tracts, had a nursing-home ministry, and regularly did everything they could with the Gospel. As a result, the glory of God was present in that church. They enjoyed the operation of the gifts of the Spirit, the power of God, the fire of God — the divine activity of the Holy Spirit. People were getting saved, discipled, and reaching out to others as the church grew not only in size, but in white-hot zeal for the things of God.

But later when the leadership began to draw back to focus on just discipleship and not on the lost, something happened. The presence and power of God that was so evident in the congregation began to wane.

In focusing lopsidedly on just maturing each other, the going of the Gospel eventually came to a standstill and stopped at this church. Little by little, the power of God began to dwindle in that church. Although the motivation to disciple was right, when they stopped "going" with the Gospel to the lost, the "lo" stopped too. The promise of Matthew 28:20 disappeared from the church in terms of God's manifested presence.

As a result of not "going," the gifts of the Spirit began to dissipate, the joy of the Spirit disappeared in the church. And that congregation that had once been so powerful became a hull of what it had previously been. And it was all connected to that moment when they dismissed "going."

God's Power Returns When We Go to the World With the Gospel

When a pastor emphasizes soul-winning — reaching the lost for Christ — that church will be filled with power. God will be with them and His presence will be experienced in that congregation of believers. What Jesus promised about being with them in power will come to pass.

There's great joy in a church that has altars packed with those who give their lives to Christ. Miracles can happen in that kind of atmosphere of spiritual fire and expectancy and zeal for the things of God. Deliverances and healings take place and financial miracles occur. The supernatural presence of Jesus spills over into the church as the catalyst that ignites and reignites fire among that congregation — all because they chose to obey His Great Commission and to "go"!

Hell Is a Real Place

People don't like to think about it, but it's a fact that hell is a real place, and people *really do go there.* J. C. Ryle writes, **"Hell, hell fire, the damnation of hell, eternal damnation, the resurrection of the damnation, everlasting fire, the place of torment, destruction, outer darkness, the worm that never dies, the fire that is not quenched, the place of weeping and gnashing of teeth, everlasting punishment — these are the words which the Lord Jesus Christ himself employs. Away with the miserable nonsense which people talk in this day, who tell us that the ministers of the gospel should never speak of hell…he who would follow the example of Christ *must* speak of hell."**

Hell is a real place. It is so real that Jesus spoke about it *three times more* than He spoke about Heaven in the Bible. He believed in the reality of hell. God is so convinced of the reality of hell that He sent Jesus to the earth to ensure people didn't go there. Jesus came to pay the price so people could receive forgiveness of sin and *not* go to hell.

C. S. Lewis said, **"There's no doctrine which I would more willingly remove from Christianity than the doctrine of hell, if it lay in my power. But it has the full support of Scripture and especially of our Lord's own words; it has always been held by Christendom and it has the support of reason."**

Hell is a central doctrine of the Bible, and when people die outside of Christ, they go there. The statistics are stark: Every day 150,000 people die. Approximately 6,400 people die every hour — that's about two people every second. Think of the stream of human beings that are leaving this life, passing into eternity, and how many of them are going into hell. The truth is, there is a funeral in every person's future as the Lord tarries His coming. That's why we have to burn with passion to make sure we take the Gospel, the best news anyone has ever heard, to every single person who is outside of Christ.

Reaching the Unsaved

Since Jesus died for this, we must live for this mission. We must reach people, and we must fund the Gospel to make sure other people hear the Good News of Jesus Christ. Today a lot of church leaders are talking about reaching unchurched Christians. That's good and right, but if no one is talking about reaching the unsaved, those unsaved people will go to hell without the Gospel.

People are in jeopardy of hell if we don't reach them. The Early Church was so infused with Jesus' teaching on hell that it gripped their hearts, and they went to the world with the Gospel because they wanted to stop people from going there. Billy Graham said, **"I am conscious of the fact that the subject of hell is not a very pleasant one. It is very unpopular, controversial, and misunderstood. But as a minister, I must deal with it. I cannot ignore it."**

This is true for every believer.

Resurrecting Corpses!

William Booth, founder of the Salvation Army, said, **"Most Christian ministries would like to send their recruits to Bible College for five years. I would like to send your recruits to hell for five minutes. That would do more than anything else to prepare them for a lifetime of compassionate ministry."**

R. C. Sproul wrote, **"God just doesn't throw a life preserver to a drowning person. He goes to the bottom of the sea and pulls a corpse from the bottom of the sea, takes him up on the bank, breathes into him the breath of life and makes him alive."**

What a miracle that God gives new life to people who are spiritually dead, and when they receive the gift of forgiveness, the gift of salvation, *immediately*, they're no longer in jeopardy of hell!

C. T. Studd said, **"Some wish to live within the sound of church or a chapel bell; I want to run a rescue shop within a yard of hell."** He believed, as others, that his job was to rescue the perishing and care for the dying. Many Christians are nonchalant about hell, *but God is not nonchalant!* He was so serious about the subject of hell that He sent Jesus into the earth to stop people from going there.

Go and *Keep Going!*

To have the fire of God raging in our hearts, we must give ourselves over to what triggers the release of that fire, including a passion for souls. when we do, we'll become infernos for Jesus!

The fuels of souls will ignite one's spiritual flame. In Matthew 28:19, Jesus said, "Go ye therefore," and the Greek literally means *go and keep going*. God's call isn't to go on one missions trip — we are to take the Gospel to others perpetually. When we go *and keep on going*, Jesus makes the glorious promise: "…And lo I will be with you always, even to the end of the age" (Matthew 28:20). God's promise to those who go, those who seek to save the lost, is that He will show up, and His presence will be with us! So we *must* "go" — it's a spiritual fuel we need to add to our fire!

STUDY QUESTIONS

Study to shew thyself approved unto God, a workman that needeth not to be ashamed, rightly dividing the word of truth.
— 2 Timothy 2:15

1. God never intended for people to go to hell, but many do because they have never heard or received the Gospel, the Good News, that because of Jesus, they don't have to go there. Jesus Christ came to earth to pay the price for sin and the redemption of mankind so people could receive forgiveness of their sins and not go to hell. Where in the Bible does it say hell is a real place? Find it and describe it. Describe how that affects you and motivates you to tell others about God's love and His redemptive plan.

2. What did Jesus mean when He says, "...And, lo, I'm with you always even unto the end of the world. Amen" (Matthew 18:20)? Explain the significance of this verse as it pertains to being a witness for Jesus?

PRACTICAL APPLICATION

But be ye doers of the word, and not hearers only,
deceiving your own selves.
—James 1:22

1. When was the last time that you witnessed to someone about Jesus' love for them? How can you show the love of Christ in your daily life so that unbelievers become open to hear the unadulterated Gospel that can save their eternal souls?

2. We simply cannot be nonchalant about sharing the Gospel. Make a commitment to speak to at least one person about Jesus this week. Note the results and follow up with that person. How did the Holy Spirit move to help you speak to that lost soul?

Notes

Notes

Notes